Public Economy and Urban Governance in China

Series Editor

Baijun Wu, East China University of Science and Technology, Shanghai, China

This book series aims to promote the research in innovation-driven development of public economy and urban governance in China, and ultimately the social governance model based on collaboration, participation, and common interests enhancing the foresight, precision, and efficiency of urban governance. Focusing on the urban governance of Chinese top megacities, this book series combines economics and sociology and explores a new way to solve problems of social governance concerning urban public goods supply mechanism, innovative models of social governance, as well as critical urban development issues like public safety, infrastructure and environmental pollution.

Chunyang Pan

Urban Infrastructure and Economic Development in China

ECUST PRESS

Springer

Chunyang Pan
School of Business
East China University of Science
and Technology
Shanghai, China

Translated by
Xie'an Huang
Graduate Institute of Interpreting
and Translation
Shanghai International Studies University
Shanghai, China

ISSN 2948-1872 ISSN 2948-1880 (electronic)
Public Economy and Urban Governance in China
ISBN 978-981-99-6628-8 ISBN 978-981-99-6629-5 (eBook)
https://doi.org/10.1007/978-981-99-6629-5

Jointly published with East China University of Science and Technology Press Co., Ltd.
The print edition is not for sale in China (Mainland). Customers from China (Mainland) please order the print book from: East China University of Science and Technology Press Co., Ltd.
ISBN of the Co-Publisher's edition: 978-7-5628-6233-8

This Springer imprint is published by the registered company Springer Nature Singapore Pte Ltd.
The registered company address is: 152 Beach Road, #21-01/04 Gateway East, Singapore 189721, Singapore

Foreword

Where Is Development Economics Heading?

About "Development Economics"

The "mystery" of economic development is always a key concern of economists and at the heart of researches on development economics. In the 1940s and 1950s, especially after World War II, a great many countries in Asia, Africa, and Latin America gained independence through tough struggles. These emerging countries soon found themselves facing the common historic task to build economic prosperity. This special history has brought development economics into being, and classic theories in this school of economics became widely known soon afterward. Arthur Lewis's "dual sector model," Raul Prebisch's "core and periphery theory," Paul Rosenstein-Rodan's "big push model" and Albert Otto Hirschman's "unbalanced growth" strategy have all promised to guide developing countries toward economic prosperity.

It is unfortunate, however, that after more than half a century since the end of World War II, few countries have properly managed the "middle income trap" and achieved sustained growth. In fact, many developing countries have stuck in long-term stagnation, and some Latin American countries have created obvious disparity between the rich and the poor and suffered from social unrest. It seems that the theories of development economics have not brought good luck to developing countries. Indian-born British economist Deepak Lal urged developing countries to return to the tradition of free market economy in his book The Poverty of Development Economics after he revealed the theoretical dilemma of development economics (Lal, 1983).

On the other hand, microeconomics and institutional economics, both based on the theory of market economy, have then prevailed and evolved into a grand theoretical system. The school of institutional economics advocated by Douglass North and Daron Acemoglu has deepened our understanding of institutions and their economic effects through wide-ranging theoretical and empirical studies. Subsequently, development economics began to merge with mainstream economic theories and models.

Gradually, it became a common knowledge that on the road toward economic prosperity, no government is "effective" without an "efficient market," but no one can ignore the country's institutional and cultural heritage, or historical background.

Judging by recent trends, development economists have turned to micro-policies to seek drivers of development. In October 2019, the Nobel Prize in Economics was awarded to American economists Abhijit Banerjee, Esther Duflo and Michael Kremer, for their "experimental approach to alleviating global poverty." A new generation of development economists, represented by these three Nobel laureates, is using randomized controlled trials to verify the positive effects of low-cost public initiatives such as increasing nutritional intake, expanding access to small and micro loans, and improving community medical care on poverty alleviation.

While they have far-reaching influence, these trials cannot take the place of studies on development economics from a macro-perspective, nor can they answer the question of whether and how public goods such as infrastructure with significant externalities will affect economic development.

About This Book

Fortunately, China's phenomenal economic development over seven decades has provided a solid basis and a valuable opportunity for reexamining the major issues of economic development. Over 70 years since the founding of the People's Republic of China, our average annual economic growth comes to 8.1%, and within about 40 years of Reform and Opening-up, the growth rate is as high as 9.4%. Just as Former World Bank Group President Jim Yong Kim pointed out in 2017, the proportion of people living in extreme poverty in the world had fallen from 40% to 10%, and China accounts for a lion's share of this change. Calculating by the World Bank's standards, the share of population living in extreme poverty in China dropped from over 80% in 1981 to below 2% in 2018. No doubt, China's economic development is highly worth study.

It is widely acknowledged that infrastructure development has played an important role in China's economic growth. In fact, in the economic history of the world, infrastructure has been deeply involved in every step forward in industrial revolution, from steam engine to electric locomotives and then high-speed trains, from radio to the Internet and then to the recent prevalence of big data, intelligence, mobile Internet, and cloud computing. In China, the rapid development of infrastructure projects, such as transportation, communication, energy, and water, has played an essential role in China's economic miracle. In a sense, China's infrastructure development itself is a miracle. So, how exactly has infrastructure development affected China's economic development is a key question that this book tries to answer.

As China enters the new era and its economy continues to grow in a "new normal" state, developing a modern infrastructure system has become an important means of upgrading China's economic development and a key to deepening its supply side structural reform. In early 2020, when the world was suddenly hit by COVID-19,

China sensitively proposed to develop 5G networks, data centers, and other new infrastructure projects in order to deal with or mitigate the impact of the pandemic. In other words, infrastructure has a more important historical role to play in the new era. Therefore, a systematic study of infrastructure and its economic effects has become the historic duty of contemporary development economists.

Overall, this book analyzes the course and achievements of China's economic development from the perspective of infrastructure, trying to identify the factors behind China's economic miracle. To be more specific, this book reviews the history of infrastructure development in China, explains the basic concepts of infrastructure, introduces the theoretical origins and mathematical models of infrastructure economics, as well as the practical economic effects and governance basis of China's infrastructure development. It must be noted that this book is not a comprehensive encyclopedia or a catalogue. It does not intend to cover all types of infrastructure, nor does it ambitiously aim to measure all effects of infrastructure or comprehensively review all historical literature related to infrastructure. Nevertheless, this book is still highly recommendable.

The value of this book rests in the fact that it focuses on history and pays close attention to the critical role of infrastructure in the global history of economic development, especially during China's economic revitalization. On the other hand, this book also faces the future, revealing the opportunities and challenges around infrastructure development in a difficult time of global economic slowdown. It goes even further to track the integration of "big data, intelligence, mobile Internet and cloud computing" in real economy. More importantly, this book focuses on China, explores the impact of China's infrastructure on market integration, open development, people's well-being, and endogenous growth, and aims to reveal the political economic logic behind China's infrastructure provision. It is our hope that this book will offer a certain level of guidance to readers to navigate the ocean of development economics and find their treasure island.

Shanghai, China Chunyang Pan

Reference

Lal, P.: The Poverty of "Development Economics". Institute of Economics, London (1983)

Foreword by Baijun Wu

After over four decades of rapid development, China has taken a brand-new look and a couple of new trends are emerging in its social and economic spheres. A remarkable economic trend is that the contribution of public goods to national economy continues to grow. After the global financial crisis in 2008, in order to prevent economic recession and maintain a relatively high level of economic growth and social stability, the Chinese government invested heavily in public infrastructure development. At the same time, in order to meet people's needs and improve social welfare in the context of urbanization and the new population policy, the government has investment more generously in public services such as education, health, safety, and social security, which has made public services much more accessible and affordable. Public goods have become an important part of the aggregate social product, and in several years investment in public goods did play a decisive role in China's marginal economic growth.

In the social sphere, while changes to the overall social structure are not obvious, new social forces generated by modern economic activities, such as the new immigrant class, the middle-income class, and private capitalists, are rising, which has a significant impact on China's economic and social development. These emerging social forces are changing the country's social structure subtly, and their impact on the balance of interests of different social groups is profound. At the same time, as the method of production and people's way of life are becoming more market-oriented and deregulated, the cultural and social needs of people have seen big changes, which creates questions about how to provide public services more effectively. In addition, driven by the transformation of productive activities and the extension of economic activities, people's mobility has been increasing, now far beyond the scope of administrative regions. Great challenges have therefore arisen, including how to update the social governance mechanisms at the community level.

These ongoing social and economic changes have created uncertainties about the future. However, overlooking political changes, we may still see a clear path of social and economic evolution. Throughout the human history, new technologies, changes in production methods and market expansion have enabled people to overcome the constraints of the natural environment and pursue a prosperous life. In this course, the private sector alone cannot guarantee a fair and safe environment for all people, while the public sector has played an essential role, under either planned economy or market economy. In one example, the provision of public goods and public services has improved the well-being of all members of society. Therefore, considering the roles of both sectors, the government must allocate resources reasonably between the private sector and public sector in the process of economic development. It must be mentioned that, in many countries where the private sector is productive, the environment is damaged, the gap widens between the rich and the poor, and social injustice worsens as the wheel of wealth creation rolls on, while the development of public goods which is intended to improve social welfare and security has met with problems such as resource shortage, inefficient supply, and bureaucracy or administrative monopoly. Therefore, people are looking for an appropriate mechanism to check excessive competition in the private sector, reduce negative externalities, narrow the gap between the rich and the poor, and always try to improve the efficiency and development of public goods through redesigning relevant institutional arrangements.

In many countries, along with the growth of economy and personal income, the role of public goods in economic and social development is gradually enhanced, and their total value and their value as a proportion of the aggregate social product are growing, which reflects the momentum of social and economic development. As is the case in many other countries, the rapid development of China's public sector after reform and opening-up is an indicator of economic and social progress. We, however, must be clearly aware that in the fast-changing social and economic environment, like the private sector, the public sector needs to address some new challenges created by disruptive technologies, changes in the marketplace and institutional transformations.

The first question is how to distribute social and economic resources between the private sector and the public sector rationally and effectively. Effective response to this challenge requires a comprehensive understanding of the real needs and effective mechanisms for resource allocation to ensure balanced supply to both sectors and meet individual and community needs, and therefore to align economic growth with social welfare, or achieve both economic efficiency and social equity.

The second is how to provide public goods more effectively. Given China's realities, we should understand and meet people's needs and preferences in theory and in practice and adopt appropriate methods to allow the public to participate in the selection of public goods and the decision-making process concerning projects to produce and deliver them. This issue involves not only a country's public goods provision, but many other factors such as politics, technology, market, and culture, while the core of issue lies in the political and economic system design. The key is to turn away from the convention that government takes care of everything and put people at the center of efforts to address their needs. The government should delegate some of its power to communities and enable social organizations to grow and play their roles in social governance. At the same time, the government should reform the government-predominated public goods provision system by remaking institutional arrangements and taking appropriate political actions and develop public goods provision system which is suitable for China and encourages multi-party cooperation.

The third is the need to create a social governance structure where everyone shoulders and fulfills common yet differentiated responsibilities, and everyone shares the fruits. The government, social organizations, and the public should be brought together under the leadership of the Communist Party of China (CPC) to form an integrated social governance system. People should be encouraged to participate in community governance, while we should try to improve the capabilities of community workers and public service providers.

Next is about how to update community governance. Social governance at the community level should be deemed as the cornerstone or centerpiece of national governance and a fundamental link in China's institutional modernization. At the same time, the government should make community governance more substantial and effective through proper institutional arrangements and legal measures, establish a governance mode that caters to the need of diversified groups, and figure out the path of administrative reform to delegate power to community organizations. At the same time, the government should build a system that enables community organizations to mobilize resources, provide public services, and make public decisions.

The last but not the least is to transform the production and provision of public goods based on new technologies such as the Internet, big data, and artificial intelligence, in order to improve the efficiency of public services and the performance of community governance. This requires continuous improvement of law so that public service providers can legally use information technologies to survey the real needs of people for public goods and services, inform public decision-making, and provide technical means for public services regulation and evaluation, which is also instrumental in fulfilling the goal of allocating resources more efficiently.

Based on the general understanding of China's long-term socio-economic trends and structural changes, as mentioned at the beginning of this preface, the Institute for Advanced Study of Social Sciences of East China University of Science and Technology has brought together a research team with a very well-defined purpose: keen observation and partial analysis of China's social and economic development at the community or micro-level. Over the years, these young professors of East China University of Science and Technology, who are also experts in public economics, sociology, and public management, have conducted extensive research on public economy and social governance with the support of international cooperation and State funding. Their efforts include: First, research on the basic theory and practices of China's public sector. Through interdisciplinary research and combining multiple research paradigms, they've dug into the relationship between and internal mechanisms of public economy and social governance in the process of social development; second, survey of new ways and new forms of public economic and social governance driven by new technologies such as the Internet, big data, and artificial intelligence; and third, field survey and empirical analysis to collect practical experiences with Chinese characteristics in order to review and revise classic theories and expand the scope of theoretical research. This series of books contains a preliminary summary of our previous research, and each book is centered around one or more the above issues.

Centering around public economics, social governance, and social policy, most of this research project studies the theory of public economics and public management as a science and explores issues of public economy and social governance in an interdisciplinary way. The studies also cover policy issues from the multi-disciplinary perspective. There are five books in this series that work on public economics. Among them, *A Research on Effective Mechanisms for Urban Public Goods Provision* surveys the research on public goods supply and discusses the mechanism of China's public goods provision and its reform, with the focus resting on the investment, financing, production, development, and access to urban public infrastructure and public services; *A Research on Urban Infrastructure and Economic Development* surveys China's achievements and challenges it has faced and still faces in infrastructure provision over the past 70 years, reveals the impact of infrastructure development on regional economic development from the perspectives of fiscal decentralization and comparative institutional analysis, conducts an econometric analysis to explore the impact of China's infrastructure development on market integration, inclusive development and improvement of people's well-being, and proposes an implementation path for reforming the model of infrastructure provision from the perspective of political economics; *A Research on the Effective Mechanism and Path for the Provision of Environmental Public Goods* studies the provision of various environmental public goods, focusing on the role and behavior patterns of households in environmental governance that people have paid relatively little attention to. With households as the main providers, intergenerational factors are included in the analysis framework, and a theoretical model of effective provision is built based on three methods for valuation of environmental public goods; based on data analytics, *A Study of the Spatial Distribution of Urban Public Services and an Evaluation of Comprehensive Service Capabilities* analyzes the development, resource scale, and spatial distribution of urban public services and service capabilities and takes stock of the factors that affect the provision of urban public services. This book then proposes strategies to optimize the provision of urban public services; interestingly, *A Research on the Multi-Party Collaborative Governance of Urban Service Sharing Platforms* focuses on the sharing economy and discusses the public nature of private goods. This book surveys the development models, governance practices, and mechanisms of urban service sharing platforms at home and abroad and proposes a coordinated multi-party governance structure in which self-governance takes the central position, while governments and communities play supporting roles. This research breaks through the traditional concepts of urban public goods provision and represents a ground-breaking study on the changes in the public consumption and production of private goods in a new tech-driven environment. To sum up, these studies focus on infrastructure development, environmental protection, pollution control, and other major public goods and public services, analyze the characteristics and mechanisms of public goods provision in China, and propose plans for institutional reform and policy recommendations to achieve effective provision of public goods.

Five other books in this series study issues of social governance in cities. *A Research on Rural-to-Urban Migrants and Public Governance* examines urban governance in the process of urbanization and studies how to shift the focus from immigration control to provision of services to immigrants in order to integrate immigrants into the urban community as soon as possible. *A Research on Urban Public Safety and the System of Risk Prevention and Control*, centering on the reality of frequent public security accidents in urban areas, analyzes the causes and types of urban public security problems, discusses how to prevent safety risks through analyzing the roots of urban safety problems, and proposes an urban security risk prevention and control model. *A Research on the Social Mechanism of Conflicts and Disputes Resolution at the Urban Community Level* takes the fast rise of mediation organizations in recent years as an example and analyzes the actual needs, capabilities, network, operation mechanism, and development logic of such organizations who stand for social forces participating in the resolution of conflicts and disputes in urban communities. In the end, it aims to proposes a social governance mechanism with Chinese characteristics to prevent social risks. *A Research on Integrated Service Models in Urban Community Governance* takes community governance practices in Shanghai as an example and investigates community governance from various perspectives such as sub-district (township) reform, government procurement of services, development of community organizations, and community participation in social governance and team building of community workers. This book then analyzes the development of social governance at the community level, reveals the new problems in community-level social governance, explores the social and structural roots of these problems, examines the elements, innovation processes, and key links of modern social governance in urban communities, and thus proposes a new concept of a social governance system at the community level in megacities. *A Research on the Development and Operation of Urban Community Development Foundations* presents an empirical analysis on the growth environment, local characteristics, governance structure, and roles of government-driven community foundations and discusses the role of such foundations. On this basis, the book proposes the development path and operating mechanism of social organizations at the community level under China's political framework.

It is worth noting that (the original Chinese versions of) these books were published at the onset of the COVID-19 pandemic. Breaking out less than 20 years after SARS, this international public health emergency once again proves the importance of harmony between man and nature and tells us that we should pay attention to the effectiveness of public health system and mechanisms, and that we should reflect on the shortcomings of the current social governance system and the possible mistakes in public policy implementation. It is gratifying to know that COVID-19 was brought under control in China shortly after the outbreak, thanks to the strict implementation of prevention and control measures nationwide, or the quick response of community organizations, which fully demonstrates the importance of establishing a multi-party supply mechanism embracing social organizations and public participation. In this sense, China's success in coping with COVID-19 also reveals the need to establish an effective public goods provision system as part of our efforts to build a modern country.

We're grateful that the publication of these books is funded by China National Publishing Fund and Shanghai's municipal publishing initiative under the umbrella of "Universities Serving Major National Strategies." We're indebted to East China University of Science and Technology Press which has managed to obtain the grants and subsidies. It also deserves mentioning with thanks that some of these books are the outcome of research projects funded by Shanghai Municipal Education Commission under its Scientific Research Innovation Program.

Shanghai, China
May 2020

Baijun Wu

Series Editor's Preface

After more than 40 years of rapid development, the economic society of China has demonstrated some new characteristics in recent years, which is mainly reflected in changes in the ways the Chinese economy is developing at the current stage. These changes often occur when economic development reaches a certain stage, partly like what happened in the history of developed countries, but with unique Chinese characteristics.

In economic growth and structural adjustment, a remarkable feature is the continuously increasing contribution made by the public goods sector to national economic growth. To counter the economic recession and maintain a fast economic growth and social stability, the Chinese government has continuously invested heavily in public infrastructure construction, particularly after the global financial crisis in 2008. At the same time, in the context of urbanization and population system reform, and the mounting needs of people's social welfare to be met, the government has increased its investment in public services, such as education, health, safety and social security, which makes the supply of economic and social public goods an important part of the total social supply. Even in some years, investment and supply of public goods have become decisive factors for economic growth.

In terms of social development and structural changes, although the overall social form and power structure has changed little, social forces, like the new emigrant class, middle income class and private capital class that came into being, as a result of modern social activities continues to grow, exerting an increasing influence on economic and social development. These emerging social forces are imperceptibly changing China's social structure and having a profound impact on the pattern of social interests. At the same time, with people's production and lifestyles becoming increasingly market-oriented and socialized, the ideas, social needs and demands of ordinary people have also undergone great changes, which adds to the difficulties in accurately grasping people's needs, preferences and behavioral changes in social governance, and poses challenges to the effective implementation of public services. In addition, with the change of production mode and the expansion of economic activity space, people's social mobility has been increasing, far exceeding the scope of administrative areas and posing a huge challenge to the traditional administrative management system and the top-down governance mechanism of the government. All these have put forward new requirements on how to reconstruct the structure and mechanism of social governance in the modern political and economic constructions.

Seen from the economic development trend of various countries, the role and status of the public goods sector in the economic and social development are gradually improving, and its asset scale and proportion in the total social supply are constantly increasing, with the economic development and the improvement of residents' income level. This reflects the state and trend of the continuous development of social economy. With a reference to the law of the development of the public goods sector in other countries, the rapid development of the public goods sector in China after the reform and opening up also reflects a regular trend of economic and social changes. However, it should be clearly realized that in the rapidly changing social and economic development environment, the growth of the private product sector will be affected by technological, market and institutional changes, and the development of the public product sector will also face many new challenges. This is manifested mainly in the following aspects:

First, how to allocate social and economic resources reasonably and effectively in the private and public product sectors. This requires a comprehensive grasp of the objective needs of the economy and society, and an effective mechanism for resource allocation to achieve a balance between the supply of the two sectors and the needs of individuals and society, and a balance between moderate economic growth and the improvement of social welfare, so as to basically achieve the two goals of economic efficiency and social equity in development.

Second, how to effectively supply public goods, especially according to China's national conditions, to solve the problems that truly show people's needs and preferences in theory and practice, adopt appropriate public choice methods, and let the public participate in the selection and decision-making system of public product projects. This problem involves a country's public goods supply system and mechanism, and political, technological, market, social and cultural factors, but the core problem lies in the arrangement and mechanism design of political and economic systems. The old stereotype of an "all-in-one government" should be abandoned, the needs of the people be truly put squarely in the center, and the government does what it should and refrain from what it should not, delegating power to the grassroots and freeing up space for the development of social organizations and their performance of social governance functions. At the same time, the government should also reform the existing government-led public goods supply mechanism through institutional arrangements and political procedures and explore a public goods supply mechanism featuring multi-subject cooperation, which is suitable for China's national conditions.

Third, how to build a social governance pattern featuring joint contribution, co-governance and shared benefits, establish a social governance community in which "everyone is responsible, lives up to their responsibility and shares in the benefits," how to establish a social governance system integrating the government, social organizations and the public under the leadership of the Communist Party of China, and how to stimulate the enthusiasm of the public to participate in community governance, and improve the ability and level of community workers and community affairs participants.

Fourth, how to innovate grassroots governance methods, which involves making social governance the cornerstone and focus of national governance and the basic link in the modernization of the national governance system and management ability. At the same time, the government must eliminate any "idle" phenomena through institutional arrangements and rule of law and establish the governance methods that adapt to multiple governance subjects to resolve administrative dilemmas of community institutions, explore de-administrative reform paths for community grassroots organizations, and build systems for resource mobilization, public service provision, and public affairs decision-making.

Fifth, how to innovate the production and supply methods of public products based on new technologies like the Internet, big data, and AI to improve public service efficiency and enhance community grassroots governance performance. This requires continuous improvement of laws and regulations, to enable public service departments to legally use IT to understand the real needs of society members for public products and services. It also provides sufficient information for public decision-making and technical means for the supervision and performance evaluation of public services, aiming to achieve effective resource allocation and supply.

Based on the above thinking and understanding of China's long-term social and economic development and structural changes, the Institute of Advanced Studies in Social Sciences at East China University of Science and Technology has formed a research team to study public economics and social governance issues in China's socio-economic development. They aim to analyze China's socio-economic development from a grassroots and microeconomic perspective in the context of the sea changes in China's society and economy. The team, composed of young teachers specializing in public economics, sociology, and public management, has undertaken quite a number of international cooperative projects and State Fund projects, focusing on three main research themes: 1. Studying the basic theory of public goods sector development and China's practice, exploring the structural relationship and internal mechanism of public economics and social governance in social development. 2. Investigating new methods and forms of public economics and social governance in the context of new technologies like the Internet, big data, and AI. 3. Conducting social surveys, field experiments, and empirical analysis in public infrastructure, public services, and community grassroots governance, aiming to find beneficial practical experiences with Chinese characteristics, review and revise classic theoretical views, and expand theoretical research scope. This series is a preliminary summary of their previous research work, with each volume reflecting these research themes.

The content of this series mainly covers the areas of public economy, social governance and social policy. Regardless of the discipline, most of the research is based on the theory of public economics and public management and discusses scientific issues in public economy and social governance in an interdisciplinary way. We also study policy issues from the perspectives of different disciplines.

Since the publication of the Chinese version, this series has received extensive attention from the academic community and society. In particular, studies on how to establish a diversified public goods supply mechanism for social organizations and public participation, and how to establish an effective grass-roots social governance mechanism have generated strong interest and triggered off more in-depth discussions. Now that the series is available in English, more readers can understand the great changes in the public economic sector and social governance in China since the reform and opening up, and understand the understanding of Chinese scholars on the practical issues of public economy and social governance. At the same time, it is hoped that scholars from all over the world will pay more attention to the reform process of China's public sector, thus promoting international academic exchanges in this field.

The publication of this series in the original has been sponsored by the National Publishing Fund and the "Publishing Project of Universities Serving the National Major Strategies." Without the support of the East China University of Science and Technology Press and the hard work of its editors, the acquisition of the fund and high-quality publication would not have been possible. The English version would never have been imagined without the constructive cooperation with Springer Nature. To these quarters, we owe our heart-felt gratitude.

Shanghai, China Baijun Wu

Acknowledgements

In this era of information explosion, it is almost impossible to complete an academic monograph all by oneself. This book is undoubtedly the fruit of collective wisdom and efforts. As it was mainly written in the most difficult period during the COVID-19 outbreak in 2020, I had kept in close touch with my collaborators in the virtual space to overcome mobility restrictions. In this sense, this book is also a product of information infrastructure.

I must thank many people who have made this book possible: Cen Xiaotian, Deng Zirui, Guo Yaming, He Lingjie, Liao Jingqing, Liao Jie, and Wang Jiasong who had collected a large amount of data and references for this writing project; Cao Zhiwei, Jiang Yunjing, and Lei Yutian who had written some parts of the first draft and later proposed many valuable revisions; and Wang Yaojia who has offered a valuable clue for designing the framework of this book based on her experience in the business world and has written several chapters.

For the completion of this writing project, I am deeply indebted to Prof. Wu Bojun who chairs the Shanghai Municipal Education Commission's Research Innovation Project "Research on the Effective Mechanism of Provision of Urban Public Goods" (Grant reference: 2017 01 07 00 02 E00008). This research is luckily funded as a part of his research project. Prof. Wu is a veteran and a fruitful researcher on China's economic development, having explored both history and theory. My discussions with Prof. Wu have benefited me a lot. Some chapters in this book are the results of my collaboration with him.

I am grateful to the Business School of East China University of Science and Technology and Shanghai Research Center for Public Economic and Social Governance for giving me access to a large amount of literature and data and a comfortable environment for writing this book. My thanks also go to the editors of East China University of Science and Technology Press for their serious, responsible, and professional editing and processing of my manuscript.

I am fully aware that this book contains errors and would appreciate it very much if any reader detects them and lets me know!

May 2020 Chunyang Pan

Contents

Chapter 1
Introduction

There is always a beginning, but few reach a fruitful end.
— Book of Songs

1.1 Motivation and Significance of Research

1.1.1 Role of Infrastructure Development in China's Phenomenal Growth

Over more than 70 years since the founding of the People's Republic of China, especially after reform and opening-up, China has scored amazing achievements in infrastructure development. Today, China boasts a transportation network that covers its entire territory, ranking first in the world in terms of both high-speed rail and expressway mileage. Even in the traditionally backward central and western regions, every county has expressway access and every village is connected by roads, which was once a wild dream. Many politicians and scholars from the developed world are awestruck by China's efficient and convenient transportation system.

Indeed, China has already completed many world-class infrastructure projects. China has eight of the top ten bridges in the world, including five of the ten longest; and the country has seven of the world's top ten ports. Looking back, in the early days of the People's Republic of China, roads and bridges were either lacking or in very bad conditions, after the lengthened wars, but now the country has become a world leader in infrastructure development.

As Chinese President Xi Jinping said, "China has made remarkable achievements in infrastructure development. Now, we boast smooth information flows, a complete and easily accessible network of crisscrossing roads, expressways and high-speed rails, high dams, West-East gas transmission pipelines, and South-to-North water transfer routes. Now, with so many vehicles, ships and planes coming and going, traveling in, to and from China has become very easy" (Xi 2018a, b). Surely, the phenomenal growth of infrastructure fully shows China's strengths, and above all

C. Pan, *Urban Infrastructure and Economic Development in China*, Public Economy and Urban Governance in China, https://doi.org/10.1007/978-981-99-6629-5_1

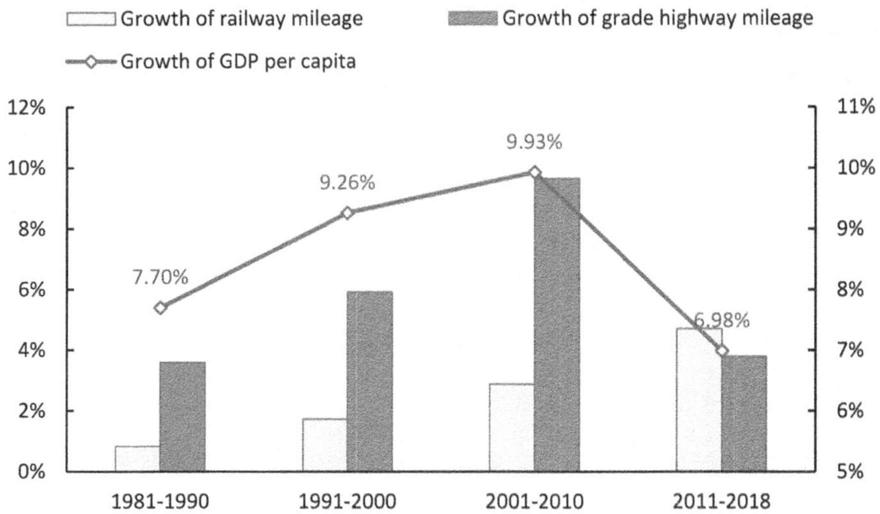

Fig. 1.1 China's infrastructure development and economic development: A comparison of growth rates. *Source* China Statistical Yearbooks

its unique advantage in mobilizing resources, which is also a key driver of China's economic miracle.

Figure 1.1 shows the growth rates of China's railway mileage, highway mileage, and GDP per capita over the past decades. Looking back at the four decades, we can see that the growth of these two most common sub-systems of transportation infrastructure matches with China's economic growth measured by GDP per capita. In other words, the speed of infrastructure growth often corresponds to the pace of economic development, as infrastructure grows faster when economy picks up speed. This may also indicate that infrastructure development has played an important role, even as a key driver, in economic development.

Railway mileage
Highway mileage
GDP per capita
Growths of railway mileage and highway mileage/%
Growth of GDP per capita/%

Governmental capital investment has always been an important source of funding for infrastructure development. Figure 1.2 shows the correlation between the growth of China's capital investment and its economic growth (real GDP growth). From 1981 to 2018, the correlation between the two rates comes to 0.80; if the history is divided into four periods, from 1981 to 1990, from 1991 to 2000, from 2001 to 2010, and from 2011 to 2018, the correlation can be as high as 0.90 during 2011–2018. These findings clearly show that infrastructure development often goes hand in hand with economic development. From 2001 to 2010, when economic growth was primarily

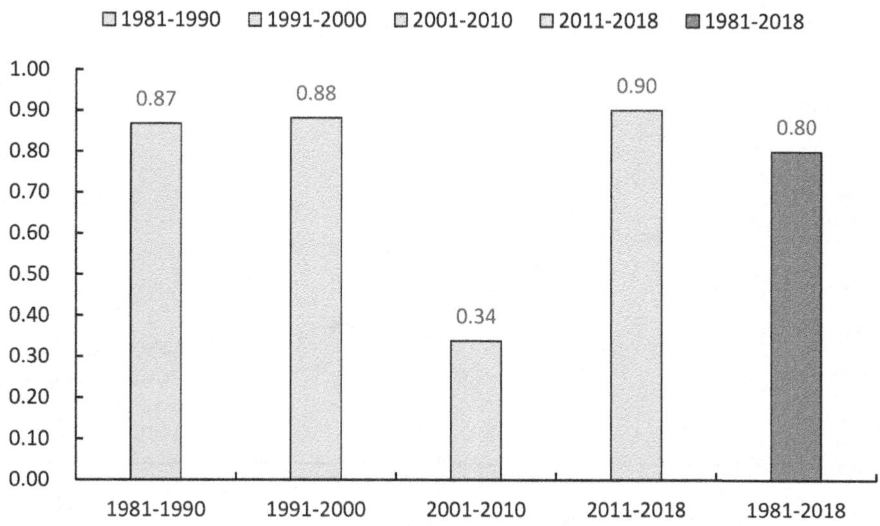

Fig. 1.2 Correlation between the growth of China's capital investment and its economic growth. *Source* China Statistical Yearbooks

driven by investment, the growth of capital investment was far higher than economic growth, resulting in a significant drop in the correlation.

1.1.2 The Middle Income Trap After a Growth Miracle

In the new era, we must be keenly aware that China is now growing in new normal state: gone are the years of rapid growth. In 2013, the CPC Central Committee concluded that China must simultaneously deal with the slowdown in economic growth, make difficult structural adjustments, and absorb the effects of previous economic stimulus policies. In 2014, the CPC Central Committee pointed out that China's economic development has entered a new normal state where the economy would face new conditions and tough challenges, so China needs to redesign its goals. Again in 2017, the report to the 19th CPC National Congress stated that China's economy was about to shift from high-speed growth to high-quality development.

Since 2007, especially after the global financial crisis in 2008, China's economic growth has fallen steadily. As Fig. 1.3 shows, the annual growth of China's economy dropped from 14.2% in 2007 to 6.1% in 2019. The decline has caused concerns about

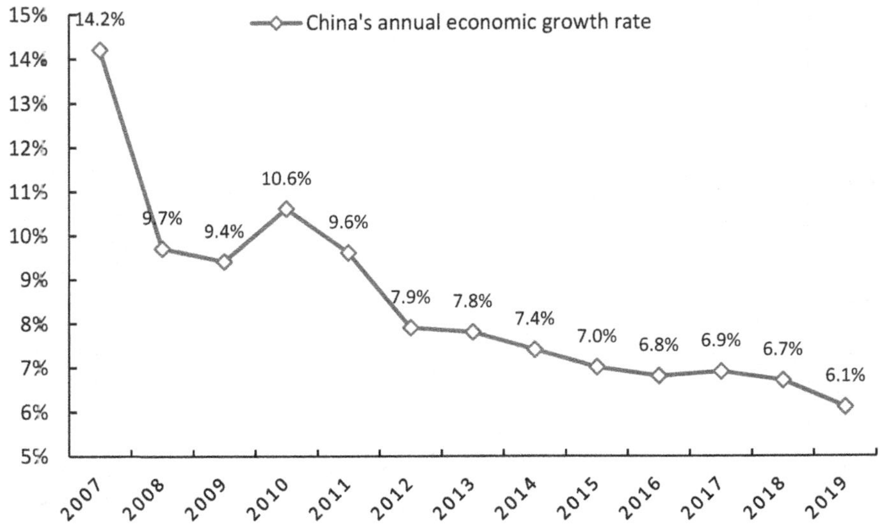

Fig. 1.3 China's economic growth rates. *Source* China Statistical Yearbooks

whether China would fall into the "middle income trap"[1] as some Latin American countries once did.

As Fig. 1.4 indicates, since the 1960s, China's GDP per capita has continued to rise, up from 89.5 US dollars in 1960 to 9,771 US dollars in 2018, but has remained below the world's average (11,298 US dollars). It means China still has a long way to go before it becomes a high-income country. Above anything else, it must try to avoid the middle-income trap.

Therefore, it is an urgent task to figure out how to avoid this trap and achieve high-quality development. The key may be found through scientific study and accurate understanding of the internal logic of China's economic downturn. Some scholars blame China's decline on the worsening external economic conditions. Since the global financial crisis of 2008, the recovery of the world economy has been sluggish, the debts of the southern European countries and some developing countries have been mounting, while trade protectionism and unilateralism have come back. Weak external demand has obviously dampened China's exports and hence China's economic growth. Other scholars, however, deem China's slowdown as something inevitable, since capital, labor and other factors of production have shown a decline in marginal output. As a general rule, after a lengthened period of economic expansion, any economy will decline, which reminds us of the "convergence hypothesis".

[1] "Middle income trap" is a concept proposed by the World Bank in its publication East Asian Visions: Perspectives on Economic Development (2006). The idea is that after the per capita income of a country reaches 3,000 US dollars, the country will fall into long-term stagnation, and will not be able to rank among the high-income countries as soon as it expects.

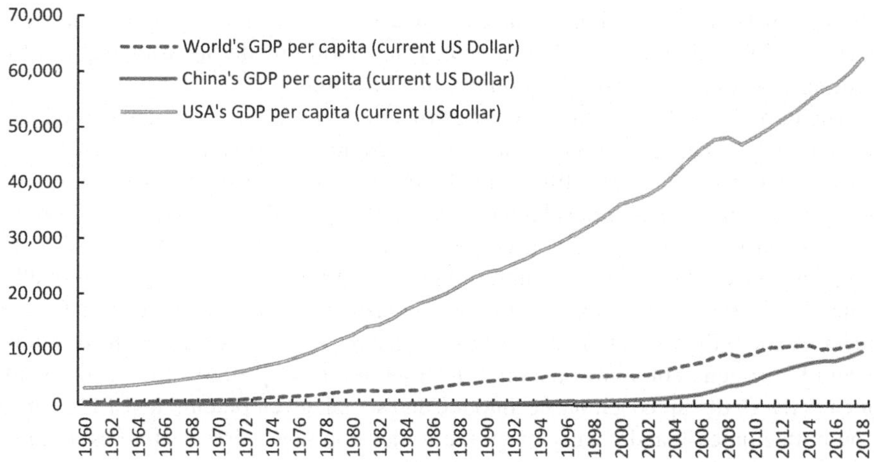

Fig. 1.4 GDP per capita of the world and China. *Source* World Development Indicators (WDI)

No doubt, both viewpoints explain the curve of China's macro economy in their own way, but there are more profound reasons why China's economy is facing pressures. This book believes that China's economic downturn not only reflects the disappearance of external momentum, but also the weakening internal drive. According to the endogenous growth theory, without exogenous forces, Total Factor Productivity (TFP) can also be driven by endogenous forces, so sustainable economic growth is still possible without external push. The power for endogenous growth mainly derives from innovations in various areas such as technology, management, and institution, and these innovations may improve TFP to different degrees. That's why China tries to shift its economic growth from a "factor input-driven" to an "innovation-driven" paradigm: China wants to keep growing in the new normal state by mastering and spearheading new trends, which is also meant to avoid the development trap and achieve sustained high-quality development.

In order to realize the shift and adjust its economic structure, the Chinese government has tried to advance the supply side structural reform, which has become its key task of economic development since the 18th National Congress of the CPC. As supply-side macroeconomic reform focuses on solving structural problems and stimulating economic momentum, through the supply-side structural reform, China intends to stimulate and capture the power of infrastructure, so the central government decided to strengthen infrastructure networks for water conservancy, railways, highways, waterways, aviation, pipelines, power grids, information, and logistics (Chen 2017). In 2018, the General Office of the State Council issued the "Opinions on Maintaining the Momentum and Filling Gaps in the Infrastructure Sector", emphasizing the need to build infrastructure projects where necessary to further improve infrastructure and public services, which also aimed at the role of effective investment in optimizing the supply structure. In 2019, the Central Committee of the CPC and the State Council jointly issued the circular entitled Outline for Building China's

Strength in Transport, stating that an extensive and powerful transportation network is essential for building a modern economy and would render a strong support for building a great modern socialist country in all respects.

The importance of building new infrastructure is more and more understood and emphasized. It is widely believed that deep integration of virtual economy (including the Internet, big data, and artificial intelligence) and real economy will become a notable trend in economic development. The 2018 Central Economic Work Conference emphasized that it is necessary to accelerate the commercialization of 5G technologies and strengthen the building of new infrastructure such as artificial intelligence, Industrial Internet, and Internet of Things (IoT). The State Council's Report on the Work of the Government also emphasized the need to strengthen the development of new-generation information infrastructure. In early 2020, after the outbreak of COVID-19 disrupted China's economic and social development, the CPC Central Committee quickly and clearly proposed to develop new infrastructure as a major measure to mitigate the impact of the pandemic. New infrastructure has not only played a unique role in responding to COVID-19 and resuming normal economic operation, but has also shown a huge potential in stabilizing investment, expanding consumption, and incubating new growth drivers.

This book studies infrastructure as an endogenous growth driver of China's economic development, and hopes to explore feasible paths to avoid the middle-income trap on the road ahead. After surveying the history of infrastructure development, basic concepts, theoretical basis, and mathematical models, this book reviews China's achievements and potential challenges the country has faced in infrastructure development from 1949 to 2019. From the perspectives of market integration, open development, people's well-being, and endogenous growth, this book then discusses the importance of infrastructure to China's high-quality economic development. Finally, this book interprets China's governance system and its impact on infrastructure provision from the perspective of decentralization, and gives policy recommendations on ways to promote the development of infrastructure like improving governance.

1.1.3 Significance of Research

This research has significant theoretical and policy implications.

First, this research carefully surveys the history, basic concepts, theoretical basis, and mathematical models of infrastructure economics to explain how infrastructure affects economic development.

Second, this research reviews China's infrastructure development from restoration and reconstruction to rapid expansion over the past 70 years since the founding of the People's Republic of China and dividing this history into two periods: the period of socialist economic reconstruction (1949–1978) and the period reform and opening-up (1978–2019). This review would give readers a deeper understanding of the significance of infrastructure to China's national economic and social development.

Third, this research empirically studies the effects of infrastructure on China's economic development, including the impacts of infrastructure on market integration, open development, people's well-being, and endogenous growth, thus informing decision-makers on how to design and adjust China's infrastructure policy to create new growth drivers and avoid any development traps.

Fourth, this research explains the significance of State governance to infrastructure provision, revealing the institutional roots of the impact of infrastructure on economic development and the direction of China's governance reform.

In short, this research aims to explain the miracle of China's economy from the perspective of infrastructure, and provide new empirical evidence to support studies on the economic effects of infrastructure in developing countries.

1.2 Framework and Method of Research

1.2.1 Framework of Research

This research centers around two core variables: "infrastructure" and "economic development".

The first part of the book, including Chaps. 2, 3 and 4, offers the theoretical basis and presents the history, basic concepts and models of infrastructure provision, major theories, empirical evidence of China and the world, and four typical mathematical models of infrastructure development. This is the starting point of research.

The second part is a historical review (Chap. 5), which covers the whole process of infrastructure development over 70 years since the founding of the People's Republic of China. This history is divided into two periods: the period of socialist economic reconstruction (1949–1978) and the period of reform and opening-up (1978–2019). This part contains the historical background, big trends, achievements, and challenges, which are presented under the classic framework of supply and demand. Historical review is the empirical basis for research and follow-up analysis.

The third part, including Chaps. 6 to 9, is dedicated to empirical research, quantitatively analyzing the effects of infrastructure on economic development from four perspectives: market integration, open development, people's well-being, and endogenous growth. This empirical research also includes causality analysis. This is the main body of this research.

The fourth part (Chap. 10), which is an analysis of institutions, explores the significance of State governance to infrastructure development, interprets China's governance system and its impact on infrastructure provision from the perspective of decentralization, and gives policy recommendations. This is the final goal of this research.

The framework of this research is shown in Fig. 1.5.

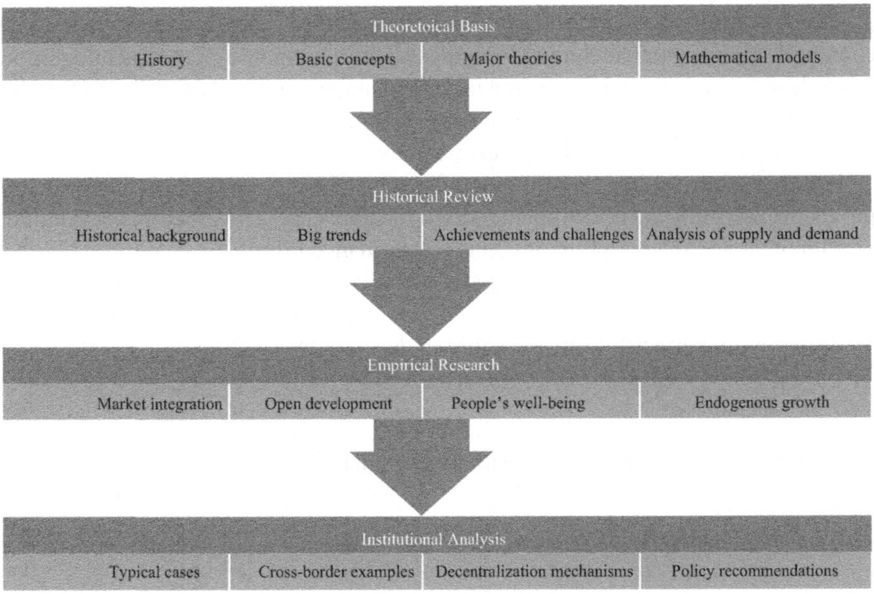

Fig. 1.5 Framework of research

1.2.2 Research Method

This research follows the classic paradigm of Structure-Conduct-Performance (SCP), but goes further by combining this paradigm of industrial economics with China's political and economic institutions and realities to form a new model of analysis: Governance-Provision-Development (GPD), thus creating a unique analytical framework.

"Governance" is the core of a country's institutional system, and in the case of China, it mainly refers to the political and economic system characterized by "political centralization and economic decentralization", which incentivizes local governments to develop and provide infrastructure. "Provision" not only refers to the type, quantity and quality of infrastructure provided by governments, but also includes the modes of infrastructure provision, such as through government procurement of services and public-private partnerships (PPP). "Development" reflects the impact of infrastructure on economic development in four dimensions: market integration, open development, people's well-being, and endogenous growth. In short, "governance" underlies "provision" which in turn affects "development".

1.3 Research Content and Key Tasks

1.3.1 Research Content

Except for Chapter 1 (Introduction), the scope of this book, or the research it represents, is as follows.

Chapter 2 first surveys the invention, evolution, and historical significance of infrastructure since the first Industrial Revolution. On this basis, this chapter presents the basic concepts, main types, and economic implications of infrastructure, and discusses the meaning and scope of "government provision of infrastructure". Finally, this chapter introduces new models of provision such partnerships between the government and the private sector, or PPP. As a Chinese saying goes, "Looking back into the past, we will understand the future better." Therefore, the history of infrastructure is the starting point for this research.

Chapter 3 first surveys the views of famous scholars and major theories on infrastructure. On this basis, it collects the empirical evidence of effects of infrastructure on economic development in developing countries in Asia, Africa, and Latin America. Then, this chapter discusses the effects of infrastructure on economic growth, poverty reduction and income distribution in China. Last but not least, this chapter examines the issues and challenges behind the effects of infrastructure on China's economic development based on literature survey. Another Chinese saying goes like this: "Other people's good practice can be borrowed to remedy one's own defects." Learning from previous researches is key to ensuring the scientific and advanced nature of this research.

Chapter 4 introduces four theoretical models of infrastructure economics and their policy implications, including the iceberg cost model, the endogenous growth model, the regional competition model, and another regional competition model that considers the externalities of infrastructure. This chapter aims to reveal the impact of infrastructure on economic growth and the underlying mechanisms by analyzing the assumptions and equilibrium results of each model.

Chapter 5 divides the Chinese history of infrastructure development from 1949 to 2019 into two broad periods: before and after the start of reform and opening-up. This chapter stands for a historical review of China's achievements in infrastructure development, and a summary of major measures and policies to bolster infrastructure. On this basis, it draws a framework of economic analysis under which it reflects on China's model of infrastructure development, as well as its achievements and challenges.

Chapter 6 explores the impact of infrastructure development on labor market integration in China via the inter-connectivity of cities through high-speed rails. This chapter proposes an econometric equation based a theoretical model that estimates the parameters using the balanced panel data of China's "city pairs" from 2002 to 2015 and the Difference in Difference (DID) method. The research finds that inter-city connectivity by high-speed rails can significantly reduce the wage gap between cities, and the effect is more pronounced between cities which are 100–900 kilometers apart, implying that the expansion of China's high-speed rail network promotes labor market integration among cities. Further research finds that the integration can be realized through increasing the flow of labor in the secondary and tertiary industries.

Chapter 7 explores the impacts of infrastructure on China's open development, especially the impact on foreign direct investment (FDI). This chapter examines the role of social infrastructure and economic infrastructure in attracting FDI inflows based on panel data of Chinese provinces and prefecture-level cities. The research finds that FDI pays closer attention to the adequacy of social infrastructure in the host city or region, and the improvement of economic infrastructure remains a positive factor in attracting FDI inflows. This chapter not only explains the regional distribution of FDI in the context of weak economic recovery in the world and China's economic structural transformation, but also informs adjustments to public policies concerning infrastructure to create an attractive investment environment.

Chapter 8 discusses the impact of clean-fuel infrastructure on people's well-being, taking the access to natural gas as an example. This chapter compares the statistics from Chinese General Social Survey (CGSS) with China's provincial macroeconomic data, and estimates people's level of well-being, or happiness, quantitatively using the Ordinary Least Squares (OLS) and the Ordered Probit models. This research finds that access to natural gas significantly improves people's well-being. Further analysis shows that access to natural gas has a more obvious effect on well-being in areas with high industrial emissions. This chapter not only explains the factors affecting the well-being of Chinese people, but also informs policies related to clean-fuel infrastructure development.

As new infrastructure is not only expected to help prevent and control the spread of COVID-19, stimulate investment and consumer demand, but also help promote China's economic transformation, Chapter 9 conducts an econometric analysis using the New Infrastructure Development Policy Index and finds that development of new infrastructure significantly raises regional economic growth and TFP. However, in regions where the economic development level is relatively low, blind development of new infrastructure may backfire.

Chapter 10 studies State governance as a basis of infrastructure provision and offers policy recommendations for promoting infrastructure development and related innovations in China. First, this chapter gives the international evidence of how governance affects infrastructure provision based on literature survey. Second, by analyzing the data of 138 developing countries, this chapter finds that good governance can help promote the private sector's participation in infrastructure. Third, this chapter interprets China's governance system and its impact on infrastructure provision, especially the impact of decentralization. Finally, this chapter offers policy recommendations on how to promote the development of infrastructure, focusing on the improvement and innovation of governance.

1.3.2 Key Tasks of Research

(1) Literature review of economic theories and models of infrastructure development

Research on the economic implications of infrastructure has a long history, dating back to Adam Smith's An Inquiry into the Nature and Causes of the Wealth of Nations (more popularly abbreviated as The Wealth of Nations), while empirical research is even more abundant and extensive. From the vast literature, this book aims to select and introduce the most representative and relevant theoretical ideas, mainly four mathematical models.

(2) Historical study of infrastructure development since 1949

Over the past 70 years since the founding of the People's Republic of China in 1949, infrastructure development in China has gone through a miraculous process from renewal of old and damaged facilities to construction of new ones, and then to leapfrog development across the board. This has happened in the broader and more glorious historical context of China's political and economic transformation. It is critical to study China's infrastructure development in this historical context. This research divides the history from 1949 to 2019 into two periods: before and after the launch of reform and opening-up, and again divides each period into several stages. Under this framework, this book analyzes the course of infrastructure development in China.

(3) Empirical study of the effects of infrastructure on economic development

Infrastructure has many types, and its impacts on economic development also vary. Therefore, it is another big challenge to decide which type or types of infrastructure should be the target of research. This book focuses on infrastructure for transportation, education and clean-fuel, and new infrastructure based on digital technologies, and explores their impacts on labor market convergence, FDI, people's wellbeing, and TFP.

(4) Institutional analysis of the impact of governance on effective infrastructure provision

Regarding the relationship between State governance and infrastructure provision, the academia has not yet reached a consensus, and there is not yet any mature analytical framework for research. Therefore, this book tries to address the above problems based on case study and borrowing from international empirical and theoretical analysis, and attempts to interpret China's governance system, especially China's style of decentralization and its impact on infrastructure provision.

References

Chen, H.: Deepening the supply-side structural reform. In: Guidebook for Understanding President Xi's Report to the Nineteenth National Congress of the Communist Party of China. Beijing, People's Publishing House (2017)

Xi, J.: Remarks of President Xi Jinping at the Ceremony Commemorating the Bicentenary of the Birth of Karl Marx. People's Publishing House, Beijing (2018a)

Xi, J.: Speech at the Celebration of the 40th Anniversary of Reform and Opening-up. People's Publishing House, Beijing (2018b)

Chapter 2
A Brief History and Basic Concepts of Infrastructure

Without it (the Pacific Railroad), the dream of traveling around the world in eighty days would always be just a dream.
– Jules Verne, Around the World in Eighty Days

This chapter first surveys the invention, evolution, and historical significance of infrastructure since the Industrial Revolution. On this basis, this chapter goes on to introduce the basic concepts, main types, and economic implications of infrastructure, and discuss the meaning and scope of "government provision of infrastructure". Finally, this chapter introduces new models of provision such as PPP. As a Chinese saying goes, "Looking back into the past, we will understand the future better." Therefore, a survey of the history of infrastructure is the starting point for this research project.

2.1 A Brief History of Infrastructure

2.1.1 Infrastructure During the First Industrial Revolution

Since ancient times, roads, bridges, rivers, and water facilities have underpinned human life, including their productive activities. Up to date, time-honored Chinese water conservancy projects such as the Beijing-Hangzhou Grand Canal and Dujiangyan are still playing a big role in water transport, flood control and irrigation, reminding us of the hard work and wisdom of the ancient Chinese people.

In the West, infrastructure facilities mushroomed during the Industrial Revolution, including the emergence of vehicles such as trains, steamboats, automobiles, and planes, along with the extending rivers and railways, the popularity of telegraph, telephone, and wireless communications, as well as the widespread application of electric energy. They have brought people closer both in time and space and accelerated the progress of human civilization.

In 1807, American engineer and inventor Robert Fulton designed a new type steamboat named "Clermont" powered by a steam engine which propelled paddle

C. Pan, *Urban Infrastructure and Economic Development in China*, Public Economy and Urban Governance in China, https://doi.org/10.1007/978-981-99-6629-5_2

wheels. Shortly after the successful trial voyage, this steamship was mass-produced and commercialized, heralding the new era of maritime transportation. Then the opening of the Suez Canal in 1869 and the Panama Canal in 1914 lifted the geographical limitation on maritime transportation and led to the formation of an international water transportation network.

In 1825, the British engineer George Stephenson drove the "Voyager" steam locomotive he designed and made a successful test-drive on a commercial railway about 48 km long from Stockton to Darlington in England. This marked the arrival of the era of railway building. After that, railways proliferated rapidly around the world and became an important alternative to the international water transportation network. By 1875, railways had been laid in all major continents: Europe, America, Asia, and Africa, which carried a total of 62,000 locomotives, 112,000 passenger wagons, and freight wagons with a capacity of about 500,000 tons. In short, the third quarter of the nineteenth century was the first age of railway (Hobsbawm 2014).

The construction of the Pacific Railroad was a landmark event in the world history of railways. In 1862, U.S. President Abraham Lincoln signed the Pacific Railroad Act which authorized the construction of a railroad that would link the United States from east to west. In 1863, the construction of the western section began, but the progress was very slow due to the rugged terrain. After 1865, the building companies began to hire Chinese workers on a massive scale. Thanks to the back-breaking labor of tens of thousands of Chinese workers, the Pacific Railway was completed in 1869, seven years ahead of schedule. This successful project facilitated the flow of production factors and the integration of markets between the east and west coasts of the United States.

While the First Industrial Revolution enabled mankind to transition from animal power to steam engine, mainly through experience accumulation and continuous efforts of skilled craftsmen, the Second Industrial Revolution brought mankind into the era of electricity through science and technology.

Since the 1830s, thanks to the unremitting efforts of British scientist Michael Faraday, Russian scientist Boris Jacobi, German engineer Werner Von Siemens, Belgian French scientist Zénobe Gramme, electric motors and generators came into the world one after another and then continued to improve, which laid a solid foundation for the electric power industry. In the 1880s, the invention and application of the internal combustion engine raised the performance of trains and ships to a new level and fueled the invention of automobiles and airplanes. In 1903, the Wright Brothers designed and built a gasoline-powered airplane, which was successfully tested at Kitty Hawk Beach, North Carolina, unfolding a new chapter of transportation. Since then, the human society had completely got rid of the slow era defined by land and sea transportation and entered the fast era marked by the seamless combination of sea, land, and air transportation.

However, the shorter spatial distance did not fully meet the needs of the human society for the rapid transmission of information. In the 1830s, American artist Samuel F. B. Morse happened to learn the principle of electronic induction during a journey, and finally invented the single-wire telegraph system in 1837. Almost at the same time, British scientists Charles Wheatstone and William Cooke invented and patented the pointer telegraph based on the principles of electromagnetism in 1837. The invention of the telegraph accelerated the dissemination of information and revolutionized the landscape of journalism. In 1876, American inventor Alexander G. Bell invented the telephone based on the principle of electromagnetic induction, and established a telephone company. In 1902, Italian engineer Guglielmo Marconi invented a successful wireless telegraph, or radio, and realized long-distance wireless communication between England and Canada. This radio "wave across the Atlantic" marked that human society had entered an era of global information exchange and real-time transmission.

In short, the first industrial revolution that began in the 1760s was not only a revolution in science and technology, but also a revolution in infrastructure.

2.1.2 Infrastructure Development Since World War II

The end of World War II was a milestone in the progress of human civilization. After the war, not only the United Nations, a supranational organization aimed at maintaining international peace, was established, but also two camps emerged, the East and the West, which were led by the Soviet Union and the United States respectively. These drastic changes in the world created a profound impact on technological advances and economic development and drove innovations in infrastructure.

Of the post-war advances in technological infrastructure, electronic computers and the Internet are the most striking examples. In 1946, the world's first electronic computer ENIAC (Electronic Numerical Integrator And Computer) was built at the University of Pennsylvania in the United States. This huge machine consisting of 17,840 electron tubes and weighing 28 tons achieved the miracle of 5000 operations per second, pronouncing the arrival of the computer age. Since then, computers have grown by leaps and bounds, experiencing four stages of development: electron tubes, transistors, integrated circuits, and ultra large scale integration. And the fifth-generation computers powered by artificial intelligence are just around the corner. Computers have been widely used in industrial, agricultural, and commercial sectors, as well as in public organizations such as hospitals, schools, and government agencies, raising the ability of human beings to organize and analyze information to a much higher level, and undoubtedly facilitating the rapid development of society in many aspects.

More importantly, the emergence of the Internet (also known as the international network) brought mankind into a new age: the Internet age. The predecessor of the Internet, the Advanced Research Projects Agency Network (ARPANET), was a project created by the U.S. military to safeguard their own computer network during the Cold War in the 1950s, and was officially launched in 1969. ARPANET was disbanded in 1989 when the process of Internet civilianization started and accelerated. Since the 1990s, industries that relied on the Internet had flourished and became an important engine for the growth of the US economy. Stock indexes such as NASDAQ 100 soared until the "dot-com bubble" burst in 2000. Nowadays, the Internet has covered all over the world, and this "information superhighway network" is growing and improving day by day, which has profoundly changed the process of human civilization.

In recent years, information technologies including artificial intelligence (AI) have developed rapidly. Computer systems equipped with artificial intelligence can replace humans in performing some intellectual activities, including perception, analysis, learning, and judgment, and are gradually put into use in scientific research and business decision-making, classroom teaching, medical diagnosis and many other fields. They are changing the industrial and economic landscape of the world at an unimaginable speed and to an unimaginable extent.

The growth of high-speed rails from invention to spread is another symbol of post-war technological development. Although standards vary from country to country, a "high-speed rail" generally refers to a railway on which trains run at more than 250 km per hour. In 1964, Japan's Tokaido Shinkansen was officially opened to traffic on the eve of the Tokyo Olympics, becoming the world's first commercially operated high-speed rail. This Shinkansen connects three major cities of Japan: Tokyo, Nagoya, and Osaka, and has driven the development of three major metropolitan area centering around these cities. The French high-speed rail network TGV opened in 1981 as the second commercial high-speed rail in the world after the Shinkansen. After that, the rapid expansion of the French TGV not only diverted passengers from air transport, but also connected the capital Paris more closely with other cities, promoting the integration of France's domestic market. The German Intercity Express (ICE) began operation in 1989. It not only covers major cities in Germany, but also runs across national borders to many cities in neighboring countries.

Now, China has overcaught them in high-speed rail network construction. In 2003, the Qinhuangdao-Shenyang Passenger Line was completed and opened to traffic, becoming the first high-speed rail in China. In 2008, the Beijing-Tianjin Intercity Railway with a design speed of 350 km per hour was put into operation on the eve of the Beijing Olympics. The momentum of China's high-speed rail construction has remained strong despite the deceleration after accidents. By the end of 2019, the total operating mileage of China's high-speed rails had reached 35, 000 km, the longest in the world. The rapid expansion of China's high-speed rail network has played an important role in promoting the flow and agglomeration of production factors.

In short, Japan, France, Germany, and China have the world's four major high-speed rail networks. These modern transportation networks have not only facilitated social and economic development within their territory, but also offered clues for addressing transportation problems in other countries and promised to promote economic development of the developing world.

No doubt, the progress of infrastructure after World War II is far more than what is mentioned above, and innovations have occurred in many spheres of modern infrastructure such as transportation, energy, communication, and water conservancy. Advanced highways, nuclear and solar energy, global satellite navigation, and water conservancy projects are major examples of post-war infrastructure development. All these types of infrastructure have provided and will continue to provide support for national economic development and social progress in different fields.

2.1.3 Historical Significance of Infrastructure Development

There is no doubt that the development of infrastructure is an important symbol of the rise of human productivity. As the Communist Manifesto says, "The bourgeoisie, during its rule of scarce one hundred years, has created more massive and more colossal productive forces than have all preceding generations together. Subjection of Nature's forces to man, machinery, application of chemistry to industry and agriculture, steam-navigation, railways, electric telegraphs, clearing of whole continents for cultivation, canalization of rivers, whole populations conjured out of the ground—what earlier century had even a presentiment that such productive forces slumbered in the lap of social labour?" (Marx and Engels 1997).

Eric Hobsbawm, one of the world's leading historians of modern times, described in detail the global expansion of railway networks since the 1850s in his book *The Age of Capital: 1848–1875*. He said, "It is impossible not to share the mood of excitement, of self-confidence, of pride, which seized those who lived through this heroic age of the engineers." (Hobsbawm 2014).

In the history of world economy, the development of infrastructure has played a significant role. First, infrastructure reduces transportation costs and shortens the distance in time and space between energy production and industrial bases, thus accelerating industrialization in all countries. As Eric Hobsbawm again said, "The characteristic products of the age were iron and coal, and the railway, its most spectacular symbol, combined both" (Hobsbawm 2014). William H. McNeill also said in his book *A World History: Interactions of Global Civilizations from Prehistory to the 21st Century* that "railroads opened up inland regions and transported large quantities of raw materials such as iron ore and coal over long distances. The Upper Silesia and Pennsylvania coalfields were mined as rail transportation opened up new opportunities" (McNeil 2013). In a word, the integration of energy and industry reduces the cost of industrial production, and promotes the process of industrialization.

Second, infrastructure expands he geographic scope of economy and connects the otherwise independent economies into a tight network, ushering in a new era of economic globalization. According to Eric Hobsbawm, "partly due to the railway, the steamer and the telegraph 'which finally represented the means of communication adequate to modern means of production'—the geographical size of the capitalist economy could suddenly multiply as the intensity of its business transactions increased. The entire globe became part of this economy" (Hobsbawm 2014). He further pointed out that, "in thirty-five years, the value of the exchanges between the most industrialized economy and the most remote or backward regions of the world had increased about sixfold. Even this is of course not very impressive by present standards, but in sheer volume it far surpassed anything that had previously been conceived" (McNeil 2013). In this sense, the development of infrastructure has played a fundamental role in economic globalization.

Finally, the development of communication infrastructure has not only accelerated the dissemination of information, but also has a strong influence on politics. In one instance, governments have nationalized telegraph businesses in order to keep in close touch with other governments and frontier outposts, or to serve their diplomatic and military needs. Meanwhile, information and communication technologies have maximized the influence of journalism, and politicians have learned to use newspapers, a traditional mass media, to influence and guide public opinions.

2.2 Concept, Types, and Nature of Infrastructure

2.2.1 Concept and Types of Infrastructure

A review of the history of infrastructure shows clearly that infrastructure does not fall into one single category; instead, it is a general concept that evolves and diversifies over time.

According to the World Bank's World Development Report 1994: Infrastructure for Development, "economic infrastructure" covers services from (1) Public utilities: power, telecommunications, piped water provision, sanitation and sewerage, solid waste collection and disposal, and piped gas; (2) Public works—roads and major dam and canal works for irrigation and drainage; and (3) Other transportation sectors—urban and interurban railways, urban transport, ports and waterways, and airports (The World Bank 1994). This World Bank report descriptively defines the concept of infrastructure through classification and illustration by example, providing a clear view of infrastructure.

The National Bureau of Statistics (NBS) of China lists "infrastructure investment" as an economic indicator and explains in this way: "Infrastructure" refers to "projects and facilities that provide basic and popular services to support social production and life, and are the basic conditions for the survival and development of society"; and "infrastructure investment" covers the following industries: rail transport, road transport, water transport, air transport, pipeline transport, multimodal transportation and logistics agencies, loading and unloading services, postal services, telecommunication, broadcasting, television and satellite transmission services, Internet and related services, water conservancy service, environment protection and governance, and public facilities. (Refer to the website of NBS for more details: https://www.stats.gov.cn.) The first sentence of the above explanation defines the concept of "infrastructure", while the second sentence lists industries closely related to or depending on infrastructure.

Chinese scholars Tang Jianxin and Yang Jun define "infrastructure" in their monograph Infrastructure and Economic Development: Theory and Policy Recommendations: "Infrastructure refers to facilities and institutions that provide common conditions and public services to support direct production activities and meet people's basic needs, and thus help achieve sustainable development goals, generally including transportation, power, communication, water supply and drainage, water conservancy and sewage facilities, as well as laws, mechanisms and systems governing education, medicine, public health, and environmental protection" (Tang and Yang 2003).

It is apparent that they have put intangible public services such as education and healthcare in the scope of infrastructure, which can be deemed as an extension of the concept of infrastructure. The academia often refers to these public services as "social infrastructure".

In Baidu Encyclopedia, "infrastructure" is defined as a broad system of engineering facilities that provide public services for social production and people's daily life, and constitute a public service system working to ensure the normal social and economic activities of a country or region. It refers to the general material condition for the survival and development of a society. This is the broadest definition of infrastructure of all.

In recent years, new types of infrastructure, or new infrastructure, have caught more and more attention. New infrastructure covers data centers, artificial intelligence, cloud computing centers, 5G mobile communications networks, industrial Internet, IoT and other systems underpinned by the Internet and digital technologies. These new types of infrastructure have played significant roles in many fields and different ways, such as speeding up information processing, raising production efficiency, improving product quality, and improving service experience. China's Central Economic Work Conference held in December 2018 stressed the necessity to accelerate 5G commercialization and the construction of new infrastructure facilities such as artificial intelligence, industrial Internet, and the IoT. The Chinese State Council's Report on the Work of the Government in 2019 also emphasized the need to strengthen and accelerate the development of "new-generation information infrastructure". New infrastructure, mainly including big data, intelligence, mobile Internet, and cloud computing, has played a unique role in the fight against COVID-19 since its outbreak in early 2020.

Another impressive benefit of developing new infrastructure is that it does not consume as much steel and cement, nor does occupy as much farmland, as traditional infrastructure facilities such as roads and bridges, although it also requires massive investment. It depends more on a country's technology strengths, including communication network and data, and other almost intangible factors of production. In other words, new infrastructure often belongs to technology-intensive IT industries and advanced manufacturing, rather than traditional capital or labor-intensive manufacturing and construction sectors.

To sum up, this book divides infrastructure into three types: economic infrastructure (traditional infrastructure such as transportation, communication, energy, and water conservancy facilities), social infrastructure (education, medicine, public health, culture, sports, and other facilities that provide daily life services), and new infrastructure (digital infrastructure such as big data, AI, mobile Internet, and cloud computing). Considering inadequate literature and data availability, this book focuses on economic infrastructure while it also makes tentative attempts to explore social infrastructure and new infrastructure.

2.2.2 Economic Attributes of Infrastructure

Although a precise definition of infrastructure is still lacking, it is not difficult to capture some economic attributes of infrastructure through the classification and examples given above.

First, infrastructure is a factor of production that connects factors of production, and is a basic condition for economic activities.

Whether it is traditional infrastructure such as transportation, communication, energy and water conservancy, or new infrastructure such as big data, intelligence, mobile Internet and cloud computing, infrastructure enables the integration of raw materials, equipment, personnel, technology, management, entrepreneurship, and other factors of production in the production sector to create value and deliver end products to the market to meet consumer needs. Along with the diversification of infrastructure facilities and the improvement of their roles, the efficiency of resource utilization (or productivity as measured by the input–output ratio) has continued to improve. Therefore, in this sense, infrastructure is a production factor that connects production factors, and is a prerequisite for various economic activities. This judgement is basically consistent with Karl Marx's description of infrastructure. In *Das Kapital: Volume* I and *Economic Manuscripts 1857–1858*, infrastructure is described as a "general condition of production". (Refer to Sect. 3.1.3 of this book for more details.)

Second, infrastructure has the character of public goods in several ways. For instance, infrastructure provision depends very much on the participation of the government.

In public economics, pure public goods are non-competitive and non-exclusive goods in principle. Non-competition means that the addition of one consumer does not prevent other consumers from benefiting from the same goods. For example, any additional vehicle does not prevent other vehicles from passing through a highway or bridge that has not yet reached the level of saturation, and the arrival of a new household in a city hardly increases the operating costs of municipal infrastructure such as gas, water, and electricity systems. In these cases, the marginal cost of infrastructure provision is zero. Non-exclusion means that it is impossible or extremely expensive to exclude any potential consumer as a beneficiary of infrastructure provision. For example, toll-free highways and bridges, free compulsory education, and many public health services are non-exclusive.

Under non-competitive conditions, if pricing is based on zero marginal cost, or provision is free of charge, it would be difficult to fan up the enthusiasm of producers, which would result in insufficient provision. On the contrary, if infrastructure provision is priced (for example, toll fees are charged for using a highway), some potential beneficiaries of infrastructure would be excluded, which would lead to underconsumption. The case is also true under non-exclusive conditions, or in cases where fee collection is not possible, such as walking on streets in towns or cities. In short, charging fees is not desirable in non-competitive cases, while it is impossible under non-exclusive conditions.

The above-mentioned problems around charging for infrastructure provision are not only typical manifestations of market failure, but also give an adequate reason for the government to assume the responsibility for infrastructure provision. Government provision of infrastructure has long been seen as the golden rule. However, due to the wide diversity of infrastructure, there are many infrastructure projects which do not fully satisfy the criteria of non-competition and non-exclusion of public goods, so there is no one-size-fits-all answer to issues concerning infrastructure provision, and the view that infrastructure provision is the sole responsibility of the government is obviously biased. To address biases concerning infrastructure provision and government responsibility in this regard, it is necessary to clear up misunderstandings of this concept.

2.3 Misunderstandings Concerning Government Provision of Infrastructure

The concept "government provision of infrastructure" is derived from the public nature of infrastructure, but due to the diversity and complexity of infrastructure projects, many people misunderstand this concept and have developed prejudices. This section presents and analyzes five major misunderstandings and tries to provide a clear view of government provision of infrastructure.

2.3.1 Misunderstanding 1: Government Provision = Free Provision

Some people argue that the government should provide infrastructure services free of charge since the government can use public funds such as tax revenues to finance infrastructure. It is true that economic infrastructure such as large-scale water conservancy facilities and urban roads and social infrastructure such as compulsory education and public health are obviously non-competitive and would benefit a huge population. The government should adopt and has adopted "financing out of tax revenues + free provision" model in these spheres.

There are, however, some situations where clear-cut solutions do not work. First, some transportation facilities such as highways and bridges involve a certain level of competition, so access completely free of charge is highly likely to cause traffic congestion and suppress the operating efficiency. Second, some public utilities such as electricity supply, water supply and central heating obviously resemble private goods, and free provision may lead to excessive consumption, thereby damaging social welfare. For such infrastructure projects and their ancillary products with apparent target beneficiaries, the government often adopts a "user-pays" provision model under the "whoever benefits pays" principle. Meanwhile, in order to meet the basic needs of the vulnerable or underprivileged populations such as the low-income people, the government implements a public welfare policy offering "partial subsidies".

2.3.2 Misunderstanding 2: Government Provision = Government Production

Some believe that "government provision of infrastructure" means that the government directly hires people to build infrastructure projects. In fact, "government provision of infrastructure" means the government use public funds such as tax revenues to finance the construction, operation, maintenance of infrastructure which are performed by contractors, while the delivery of services that infrastructure provides to consumers depends on businesses, hospitals, schools, communities, and other market entities. In short, "government provision of infrastructure" involves "market production + government payment".

Therefore, behind "government provision", there is a giant network responsible for infrastructure production consisting of countless market entities such as companies, public institutions, private organizations (including private non-enterprise entities and foundations). In terms of industrial mix, there are not only manufacturing, construction, and extractive companies, but also service providers such as education, medical care, public administration, and scientific and technological research and development institutions. There is fierce competition among these entities, which not only helps guarantee the building efficiency, functional innovation, and quality of infrastructure projects, but also helps the government find the best contractors through competitive bidding. In short, government provision of infrastructure also depends heavily on the market.

2.3.3 Misunderstanding 3: Government Provision = Sole Source

Some people believe that, considering the nature of private capital and its inherent purpose to seek profits, any private entity should not be directly responsible for providing infrastructure, so the government becomes the sole provider of infrastructure. Although the government plays an irreplaceable role in providing infrastructure, there are diversified practices or ways to fulfill this role.

Since the mid-1980s, partnerships between the government and the private sector to provide infrastructure have emerged and have been gradually popularized. The models of public–private collaboration include Build-Operate-Transfer (BOT) and Build-Own-Operate (BOO). These models of PPP not only leverage the relative advantages of different parties or entities especially the wide-ranging professional skills and flexible operation mechanisms of the private sector, but also help reduce the cost of government regulation and improve administrative efficiency. In short, these innovative models can mobilize both the government and businesses, and is becoming the mainstream model of infrastructure provision.

2.3.4 Misunderstanding 4: Government Provision = Universal Satisfaction

Some people believe that since the government often sets uniform standards for the quantity and quality of infrastructure provision, people would feel the same level of satisfaction with infrastructure, or in other words the fairness of infrastructure provision would be guaranteed. In fact, however, different users have different perceptions of the same infrastructure. To put it in another way, different users have different demand curves for infrastructure, so uniform provision of infrastructure by the government does not mean that all users would be equally satisfied.

Take the massive construction of urban expressways and rail transit in some cities in recent years as an example. Although every urban resident has equal access to these transportation facilities, those who have frequent commuting needs are clearly more satisfied and give more positive feedback than those who work from home and retirees. If the commuters are divided, driving commuters will give a higher rating of wide and smooth expressways, while those who take public transport would speak more favorably of rail transit better that extends in all directions.

This suggests that implementing unified standards of infrastructure provision is only the starting point, and there is a long way to go before the people's growing needs for a better life can be met. Facing the diversity of infrastructure needs, the government must perform timely collection and accurate analysis of user information which are critical to the development of effective policies, but test the government's administrative capability.

2.3.5 Misunderstanding 5: Government Provision = Willingness to Provide

Some take it for granted that the government is willing to provide infrastructure. This belief reflects the confusion between fact and opinion. In fact, the idea that the government should provide infrastructure is an opinion and policy recommendation of scholars based on the theory of public economics. This recommendation does not necessarily mean that government officials are willing to provide infrastructure. According to the theory of public choice, government is not a "charity organization" that aims solely to maximize social welfare. Government officials, like manufacturers and consumers, are rational people who would respond actively to incentives and try to avoid harm.

Under the traditional evaluation mechanism centered on economic growth, local government officials are often incentivized to provide highways, public utilities and other infrastructure projects that can drive economic growth in the short term, preferably within their term of office, while relatively speaking there is a lack of willingness to provide social infrastructure such as basic education, medicine, and public health, or develop new infrastructure to promote economic transformation. What is even more worrying is that in some poverty-stricken areas, local government officials are not even willing to provide the most basic infrastructure such as roads, water supply and electricity; instead, they would rather try to keep their "title" as "poverty-stricken counties" to feed on financial subsidies from the central government.[1] Since the 19th National Congress of the CPC, as China's official evaluation system keeps improving and the targeted poverty alleviation policy unfolds, the above problems have found remedies. In a word, only an appropriate incentive mechanism can truly make public service a real commitment of government officials that will be delivered.

2.4 Innovations in Infrastructure Provision Models

For a long time, the investment, construction, operation, and management of infrastructure have remained the exclusive rights of government departments and state-owned enterprises due to high cost, long payback time and low returns on investment. After World War II, the governments of many industrialized countries were forced to own and run banks, airlines, steel companies, railroads, military industries, or postal and telephone companies. However, a great many facts have shown that the government was typically unable or unwilling to run public enterprises on commercial terms, so the operating inefficiencies and losses of public enterprises were very common (Tanzi and Schuknecht 2000). Faced with this difficult situation, it was a common practice for governments to give subsidies to state-owned enterprises from fiscal revenues, which in turn resulted in soft budget constraints on state-owned enterprises. Given the government's financial support, the heads of state-owned enterprises were even less motivated to improve their operational efficiency; instead, they pursued luxuries paid for by their enterprises, which eventually worsened their losses. In this way, many countries have accumulated debts as their budgets expanded. Some have even fallen into a vicious circle of "the more losses, the more subsidies, and the more subsidies, the more losses."

Beginning in the 1980s, economic liberalism rose to prominence in macroeconomics around the world. On the one hand, the "New Public Management Movement" surged which aimed to improve administrative efficiency and rationalize the

[1] In March 2012, the Chinese central government updated the list of State-level poverty-stricken counties. While 38 counties (or districts) were deleted, the total number in each province remained stable, with a new county was picked to fill the gap of any deleted one.

government. On the other hand, the "privatization movement" aiming to promote free competition and let the market play a bigger role was gaining momentum. The Reagan administration of the United States attempted to boost its economy by cutting government spending and reorganizing public enterprises. The Thatcher government of the UK cut the public sector dramatically and worked to privatize British State-owned enterprises.

In this context, the privatization of infrastructure became an important means to shift government functions and improve the efficiency of public spending. The private sector rose quickly to the opportunity of participating in the provision of infrastructure, and a number of innovative models of infrastructure provision emerged, mainly including BOT. BOT is an infrastructure provision model in which the government gives concession rights to a company to build an infrastructure project within a certain period of time, after which the company would be responsible for its operation, and then transfer the project ownership to the government after the license terminates.

Later, BOT gave rise to quite a few derivative models, such as: Operation and Maintenance (O&M), Management Contract (MC), Lease-Operate-Transfer (LOT), Build-Operate-Own (BOO), Buy-Build-Operate (BBO), Transfer-Operate-Transfer (TOT), Rehabilitate-Operate-Transfer (ROT), Concession, and combinations of the above models. (Refer to the website of China Public Private Partnerships Center: https://www.cpppc.org.)

These models in which the government signs long-term contracts with the private sector to jointly provide infrastructure and other public goods or services are collectively referred to as Public Private Partnerships (PPP). Although various PPP models have different pricing mechanisms, returns on investment, risk sharing ratios, and termination clauses, it is important that the government and businesses agree on a contract mechanism for benefit sharing, risk sharing, and long-term cooperation. The privatization of infrastructure has not completely removed the government's role in providing infrastructure, but has transformed the nature of government, freeing the government from directly organizing production and financing and allowing it to focus on regulating activities in this sector.

Since the 1990s, PPP has gradually prevailed in developing countries where the demand for infrastructure is huge and the government's financial capacity is limited. Figure 2.1 shows the changes in total investment in infrastructure with private participation (or private participation in infrastructure, PPI) in energy, communications, transport, and water supply and sanitation in developing countries since 1996. PPI experienced a decline after reaching a historical high around 1998, but after 2002, investment in the first three categories climbed up steadily, while investment in water supply and sanitation has remained stable. Since the global financial crisis in 2008, investment in communications infrastructure rose first and then dropped, while investment in energy and transportation infrastructure continued to rise, fluctuating only after 2012. In conclusion, PPP has played a more and more important role in the financing, construction, and operation of infrastructure projects in developing countries.

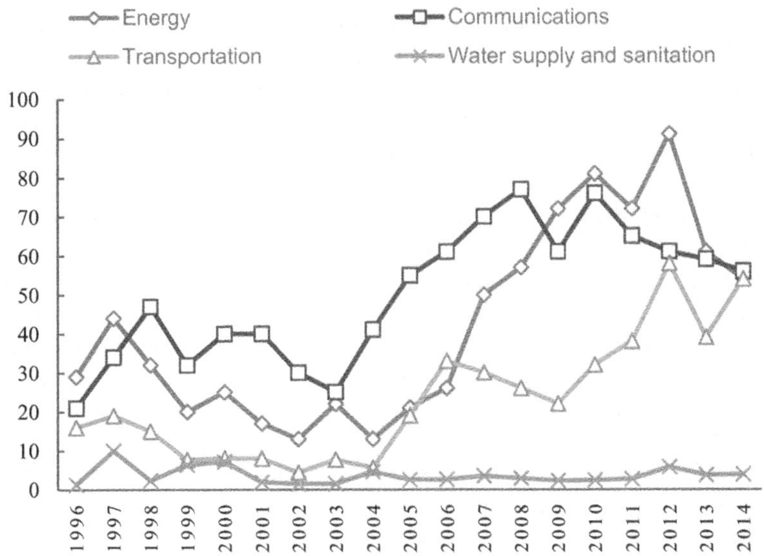

Fig. 2.1 Changes of total investment in infrastructure with private participation in developing countries. *Source* World Development Indicators database

References

Hobsbawm, E.: The age of capital: 1848–1875. Translated by Zhang Xiaohua et al. Beijing, CITIC Press (2014)

Marx, K.H., Engels, F.: The communist Manifesto. Translated by the Compilation of the works of Marx, Lenin and Stalin by the Central Committee of the Communist Party of China of the Communist Party of China Bureau. Beijing, People's Publishing House (1997)

McNeil, W.H.: A World History: The Interaction of Global Civilizations from Prehistory to the 21st Century. CITIC Press, Translated by Shi Cheng and Zhao Jing. Beijing (2013)

The World Bank: World Development Report 1994: Infrastructure for Development. The World Bank, Washington (1994)

Tang, J., Yang, J.: Infrastructure and Economic Development: Theory and Policy Recommendation. Wuhan University Press, Wuhan (2003)

Tanzi, V., Schuknecht, L.: Public Spending in the 20th Century: A Global Perspective. Cambridge University Press, Cambridge (2000)

Chapter 3
Origin and Development of Infrastructure Economics

I once tried standing on tiptoe and gazing into the distance, but I found I could see much farther by climbing to a high place.
– Xunzi, Encouraging Learning.

This chapter first surveys the views of famous scholars and major theories on infrastructure. On this basis, it collects the empirical evidence of effects of infrastructure on economic development in developing countries in Asia, Africa, and Latin America. Then, it focuses on the impacts of infrastructure on economic growth, poverty reduction and income distribution in China. Finally, it reflects on the issues and challenges China must address concerning infrastructure based on literature survey. As another Chinese saying goes, "Other people's good practices can inspire one to remedy his own defects." It is hoped that learning from previous research would ensure the scientific and advanced nature of the research presented in this book.

3.1 Previous Studies on Infrastructure Economics

Research on infrastructure economics has a long history. Many famous economists have carried out in-depth and extensive research on the two fronts: the economic effect of infrastructure and the models of infrastructure provision, and they have drawn a series of enlightening conclusions.

3.1.1 Adam Smith's Theory of State Functions

Research on infrastructure economics can be traced back at least to the theory of the functions of the State proposed by Adam Smith, father of modern economics and the pioneer of classical liberal economics. In his pioneering work on economics, *The Wealth of Nations*, published in 1776, Adam Smith argued that a government should undertake three major functions: the duty of protecting the society from violence and

C. Pan, *Urban Infrastructure and Economic Development in China*, Public Economy and Urban Governance in China, https://doi.org/10.1007/978-981-99-6629-5_3

invasion of other independent societies; secondly, the duty of protecting, as far as possible, every member of the society from the injustice or oppression of every other member, or the duty of establishing an exact administration of justice; thirdly, the duty of erecting and maintaining certain public works and certain public institutions which it can never be for the interest of any individual, or small number of individuals, to erect and maintain national borders (Smith 2008). In his statement, "public works" include physical works like good roads, bridges, navigable canals, and harbors, as well as public facilities for education and religion. Adam Smith emphasized that the construction and maintenance of public works would facilitate the commerce of any country.

At the same time, Adam Smith also examined the models of public infrastructure provision. He believed that, on the one hand, as public works benefit the local area only, they should be financed from local tax revenues and managed by local governments. Although there may be local governments abusing tax revenues, such abuses are far less serious and much easier to prevent or rectify than abuses by the national government. To put it in today's economic terms, infrastructure should be provided by local governments, a model called "decentralized provision". On the other hand, public infrastructure can be financed using the "whoever benefits pays" model, which ensures fairness in financing. Therefore, infrastructure can also be provided by the private sector, rather than the government using tax revenues.

It is awesome that Adam Smith had proposed the models of "decentralized provision" and "private provision" more than 240 years ago, which proves his foresight and sagacity in economics.

3.1.2 Friedrich List's "Standard Model"

Friedrich List was a skeptic and critic of classical liberal economics, and a pioneer of the German historical school. In his theory, the government should play a leading role in economic activities, contradicting the classical liberal economic principle of minimal or limited government that a government is best which governs least.

It must be noted, however, that concerning infrastructure provision, Friedrich List gave basically the same policy recommendations as those of the classical liberalists. In his theory of governmental interference, Friedrich List emphasized that it is the duty of the government to build infrastructure such as roads, railways, bridges, canals, and sea walls. In short, the government shoulders the responsibility to increase the productive capacity and wealth of a nation and to transform the nation from the lowest state of barbarism into a state of civilization and the highest possible prosperity, and from a state of weakness to a state of great power.

In his book *Global Economic History*, Robert Allen, contemporary global economic historian and professor of Oxford University, systematically reviewed the roads to economic prosperity in Russia, Japan, Mexico and other countries since the late eighteenth century, finding that building railways, unifying tariffs, establishing banks, and developing education are four major forces driving economic prosperity, which he called the "standard model" (Allen 2008).

In the 1830s, Friedrich List was actively engaged in the construction of railways in Germany, but unfortunately, he was expelled by the German government for his part in a financial scandal. In 1841, Friedrich List published his book *National System of Political Economy*, which established his position in the history of economics (Blaug 2015).

3.1.3 Karl H. Marx's "General Conditions of Production"

Karl H. Marx was the revolutionary mentor of the proletariat and all working people around the world, creator of Marxism, the co-founder of international communism. To date, Marxism is still highly relevant (Xi 2018).

Karl Marx had examined the connotations, functions, and provision models of infrastructure. In his masterpiece on economics, *Das Kapital: Volume I*, Karl Marx said, "In a wider sense we may include among the instruments of labour, in addition to those things that are used for directly transferring labour to its subject, and which therefore, in one way or another, serve as conductors of activity, all such objects as are necessary for carrying on the labour process. These do not enter directly into the process, but without them it is either impossible for it to take place at all, or possible only to a partial extent … Among instruments that are the result of previous labour and also belong to this class, we find workshops, canals, roads, and so forth" (Marx et al. 2004). In his words, "All such objects as are necessary for carrying on the labour process" include infrastructure, which is an essential condition of labor and production, and thus one of the determinants of productivity.

In his *Economic Manuscripts of 1857–1858*, Karl Marx divided the conditions of production into "particular conditions of production" and "general conditions of production". The former the conditions prerequisite for the immediate production process and applicable in the production process of individual capitalists. The "general conditions of production" refer to roads, canals and other material conditions that facilitate circulation, fixed capital in the form of railways, buildings, agricultural facilities, drainage works, and the production sector that builds and operates railways, canals, water supply, telegraph, and other fixed capital (Marx and Engels 1979). Karl Marx then described the three major functions of the general conditions of production: one is to facilitate circulation, the second is to make circulation possible, and the third is to increase the force of production. In a word, the general production conditions categorized by Karl Marx correspond to the modern concepts of infrastructure, which is not only a necessary condition for production activities, but also a driver for social development.

It is worth noting that Karl Marx also examined the models of infrastructure provision. He believed that there are three ways to provide roads: by means of the corvée, through taxes, and by individual capitalists. The first two ways are public models of infrastructure provision. As Karl Marx said, it is "a forced transformation of a part of a country's surplus labour or surplus product into roads." The last one is equal to private provision of infrastructure. When the capitalist economy is highly developed, capital is concentrated in the hands of private capitalists, and capitalists are allowed to charge fees for using roads and bridges, capitalists would be able and motivated to undertake infrastructure provision.

Karl Marx further pointed out, "A country, e.g., the United States, may feel the need for railways in connection with production; nevertheless, the direct advantage arising from them for production may be too small for the investment to appear as anything but sunk capital. Then capital shifts the burden on to the shoulders of the state; or, where the state traditionally still takes up a position superior to capital, it still possesses the authority and the will to force the society of capitalists to put a part of their revenue, not of their capital, into such generally useful works, which appear at the same time as general conditions of production" (Marx and Engels, 1979). Therefore, in Karl Marx's view, the state has the duty and ability to provide infrastructure for society, which is basically consistent with Adam Smith's theory of state functions and Lister's theory of state intervention.

3.1.4 John Keynes' "Aggregate Demand Management"

John Maynard Keynes was a world-renowned British economist widely hailed as the "father of macroeconomics". His masterpiece, T*he General Theory of Employment, Interest and Money*, initiated the so-called "Keynesian Revolution" of economics, challenging the predominant laissez-faire economic policy at that time, and proposing a system of theories and policy recommendations on how to deal with economic recession and achieve economic prosperity. Aggregate demand management and government interference constitute the core of his theory.

As should be pointed out, though John Keynes did not conduct any specific research on infrastructure, he regarded infrastructure construction as an important means of government intervention in the economy. He believes that in the period of economic recession, the total demand is seriously insufficient and the unemployment rate remains at a high level. At this time, the government can recruit a great many unemployed personnel with compensations to construct infrastructure such as roads and bridges. These employees will increase consumption through their income, thereby stimulating corresponding production departments to hire workers and expand output. Such newly employed will bring a new round of consumer demand and provide stimulus for a new round of employment. Therefore, the economy will go out of recession and move towards prosperity in a cycle. John Keynes called the foregoing effects the "multiplier effect". In some economics textbooks, the above-mentioned logic is pushed to the extreme; for the purpose of expanding consumption and boost the economy by artificially creating employment opportunities, we can employ two hundred people to dig a pit, and hire another two hundred people to fill the pit. This "pit-digging proposal", though biased, does reflect the essence of Keynesianism.

In the 1930s, the Keynesian approach helped the United States out of the Great Depression. In 1933, US President Franklin D. Roosevelt signed the "New Deal" which revived the economy in the Keynesian way, creating a paradigm of state interference in economic activities. The New Deal involved hiring unemployed Americans to build a wide range of public facilities including schools, bridges, dams, sewer systems, post offices and administrative offices. The most famous example is the development of the Tennessee River Basin. It is therefore apparent that infrastructure not only plays a positive role in creating and sustaining long-term economic prosperity, but also offers a feasible tool to end economic recessions quickly.

3.1.5 Development Economics Concerning Infrastructure

After World War II, many third-world countries became independent, but afterwards they faced the urgent task to achieve economic prosperity as soon as possible. Luckily, they got vital clues from development economics.

In his book *Stages of Economic Growth: A Non-Communist Manifesto*, American economic historian Walt Whitman Rostow reviewed economic history of the West from take-off to maturity, and argued that the socio-economic development of a country can be divided into six stages: the traditional society, the preconditions for take-off, the take-off, the drive to maturity, high mass consumption, and beyond consumption (Rostow 2001). Through this model, he stressed that investing heavily in infrastructure is an essential condition for developing countries to achieve economic take-off.

Albert O. Hirschman, a famous American development economist, put forward the strategy of unbalanced growth. He argued that the government should focus on supporting key sectors or companies, which would create positive externalities through cross-sectoral linkages, thereby promoting across-the-board development. In this way, economic development is like a "chain" running from the leading sector to other sectors in a country. Generally speaking, the government should give priority to investment in infrastructure projects that take long periods to complete, require massive funding, produce low short-term yields, and have high correlation with other sectors. Investment in such projects would reduce the costs of downstream manufacturing industries (forward chaining). At the same time, it also expands the demand for energy supply and construction firms (backward chaining). Through these effects combined, investment in infrastructure would ultimately drive a country's economy towards prosperity (Hirschman 1991).

Another renowned British development economist Paul Rosenstein-Rodan put forward "the theory of big-push" (Roland 2016). He held that all economic sectors of a country support and depend on each other, just like the body and the wheels of a car. Only when they are proportionate and work with each other can they "drive" with power and speed. For example, infrastructure and the private sector may not be linked at first glance. However, without the government providing infrastructure such as roads, ports, and airports, the private sector could not transport goods. They simply cannot invest in any area where infrastructure is lacking. Infrastructure and the private sector are independent from each other in a free market system where it is difficult to align their goals. To solve this problem, the governments of developing countries should play a bigger role in infrastructure investment and provision. In conclusion, development economists unanimously support government investment in infrastructure.

3.1.6 The Public Goods Theory

Since the 1960s, different schools of economics have converged, with classical liberalism, radicalism and conservatism blended to form a new mainstream school called the "Neo-classical Synthesis" (also referred to as the neo-Keynesian theory). The Neo-classical Synthesis looks at infrastructure from the perspective of public goods. It no longer emphasizes the importance of infrastructure for economic development, but instead focuses on the models of infrastructure provision.

This new school believes that a perfectly competitive market does not exist, and any market has some defects which will lead to market failure and damage the efficiency of resource allocation. Public goods are one of the causes of market failure. According to the analysis above, public goods face a dilemma: charging the provision of public goods would lead to insufficient demand, while free provision would lead to insufficient supply. In a word, the emergence of public goods leads to market failure and undermines the efficiency of resource allocation by market.

Evidently, infrastructure projects such as roads, bridges, ports, and lighthouses basically conform to the characteristics of public goods. Therefore, it is natural to study infrastructure from the perspective of public goods. Representative of the neoclassical synthesis school and winner of the Nobel Prize in Economics in 1970, Paul A. Samuelson, known as "the last generalist in economics", published his famous essay *The Pure Theory of Public Expenditure*, which pointed out that under non-competitive conditions, people are motivated to conceal their true preferences for public goods, so no decentralized pricing system can serve as an effective solution for public goods allocation (Samuelson 1954). Therefore, the government's responsibility to provide public goods has become the golden rule to solve the above-mentioned market failures.

After the 1980s, this "golden rule" was challenged by the new institutional school. Ronald H. Coase, founder of the Neo-institutional School of economics, co-founder of another new school of economics: "law and economics", and winner of the 1991 Nobel Prize in Economics, argued in his famous, *The Lighthouse in Economics*, published in 1974 that though Samuelson and other important scholars have come to the conclusion that "the impossibility of securing payment from the owners of the ships that benefit from the existence of the lighthouse makes it unprofitable for any private individual or firm to build and maintain a lighthouse" based on the theory of public goods, they are contrary to historical facts (Coase 1974). Ronald Coase investigated the British lighthouse system and found that in the early seventeenth century, the Trinity House built two lighthouses and had the privilege to build lighthouses. However, from 1610 to 1675, the Trinity House did not erect any lighthouse, while private individuals built ten instead. The tolls were collected at the ports by agents who might be private individuals but were commonly customs officials. The toll varied with the lighthouse and ships paid a toll, varying with the size of the vessel, for each lighthouse passed. It was normally a rate per ton for each voyage. After 1820, the Trinity House began to purchase private lighthouses and turn them into public lighthouses. This move was not implemented because of the difficulty in charging lighthouses, but because the government believed that private lighthouses were too expensive and there was need to lower lighthouse duties. Ronald Coase's "lighthouse" is not only a historical example of private provision of infrastructure, but also a beacon of the coming of the property rights theory.

Joseph E. Stiglitz, a neo-classical synthesis economist and winner of the 2001 Nobel Prize in Economics, mentioned the "lighthouse" issue in his book *Economics of the Public Sector*, arguing that a large shipowner with many ships might provide lighthouses but it would only consider his own benefits, not the benefits received by others, so even if they were willing to provide lighthouses, the lighthouses would be insufficient and inefficient (Stiglitz and Rosengard 2015).

3.1.7 Robert W. Fogel's "Counterfactual Analysis"

Robert Fogel deserves a place in the history of infrastructure economics. As a famous economic historian and winner of the 1993 Nobel Prize in Economics, Robert Fogel is known for his research in Cliometrics.[1] In the 1960s, he studied the economic effects of building the railroad network in the US in the second half of the nineteenth century, leading to the publication of *Railroads and American Economic Growth: Essays in Econometric History*. In his research, Fogel (1964) creatively raised a "counterfactual" question: If the United States had not built railroads at that time, what would be its economic growth rate? It is imaginable that if the "counterfactual" growth rate is close to the real growth rate, it could be concluded that railway construction did not contribute to economic growth, which would be undoubtedly counterintuitive.

Robert Fogel believed that if there were no railroads, people would use roads and waterways (rivers and canals) as alternative means of transportation. Based on this hypothesis, he found through complex calculations that the "social savings" generated by railroads were equal to about 1.8% to 3.1% of the U.S. gross domestic product. He believed that this percentage is rather small. If there were no railroads, the U.S. economy would have been delayed by only two years at most. Therefore, the contribution of railroads to the U.S. economy had been significantly overestimated. Of course, Robert Fogel admitted: On the one hand, as the railway network grows

[1] The word "cliometrics" is composed of two parts: "clio" and "metrics". The former is the name of the goddess Clio who was in charge of history in Greek mythology, and the latter means to measure.

denser, the cost of rail transportation would continue to drop, even below the cost of water shipment; on the other hand, it is precisely because the United States has a developed water system that such a "counterfactual" estimate would be possible. It would not work for the UK or Mexico.

For a time, Robert Fogel's research aroused an uproar, and many economists raised doubts about his research conclusions and methods (Sui 2009). Today, the conclusions of Robert Fogel may seem insignificant, but it must be admitted that his "counterfactual" thinking has a strong influence on later scholars who examined the causal effect of infrastructure. Robert Fogel's courage to challenge traditional concepts and well-accepted conclusions is an invaluable asset of the academic community.

3.2 Economic Development Effects of Infrastructure in Developing Countries

Any theoretical study of how infrastructure affects economic development cannot be substituted for empirical research based on real data. Over the long past, economists have studied the impact of infrastructure on productivity, economy, and poverty using various research tools such as econometric models, and have drawn a series of enlightening conclusions.

David Alan Aschauer's famous 1989 paper "*Is Public Expenditure Productive?*" (Aschauer, 1989) is a major outcome from earlier study of the effects of infrastructure on economic development. David Aschauer analyzed the data of the United States from 1949 to 1985, and found that non-military public investment has a positive impact on productivity, while spending on "core public goods" such as roads, highways, airports, transportation hubs, sewers, and water supply facilities is statistically significant in explaining the level of productivity. Based on this, David Aschauer insisted that the decline in labor productivity in the US since the 1970s had been caused by a decline in public expenditure on infrastructure. Although it focused on a highly developed country, this paper has subsequently led to a series of similar studies in developing countries. Studies on developing countries in Asia, Africa and Latin America generally have shown that improving infrastructure has important practical significance for increasing productivity, promoting employment, and eradicating poverty.

3.2.1 Empirical Evidence from Asian, African, and Latin American Countries

In his research on Vietnam, van de Walle (1996) analyzed data from the Living Standards Survey covering 4,800 Vietnamese households (23,790 persons) from the year 1992 to 1993. He found that infrastructure has a redistributive effect. Providing irrigation infrastructure to poor households with relatively less land per capita is conducive to increasing their crop income, while the economic return on investment in irrigation infrastructure can reach at least 20%. Larsen et al. (2004) analyzed the data of public investment projects in Vietnam from the year 1993 to 2002. They found that public investment in infrastructure has made a huge contribution to poverty alleviation in Vietnam, which is mainly due to the improvement of infrastructure quality rather than the increase of quantity. Meanwhile, the improvement of transportation, water supply and sanitation are more effective for poverty alleviation.

Indian infrastructure has been a hot issue of study in development economics. Donaldson (2018) examined the impact of railroad construction on inter-regional trade in colonial India. Guided by predictions from a general equilibrium trade model, and analyzing trade data for 17 commodities across 45 regions in India, he found that railroads lowered trade costs and interregional price gaps, which not only increased inter-regional and international trade, but also increased real income levels from agriculture. As the construction of railroads may be selective, that is, the authorities may choose to build railroads in areas with greater economic potential, the effects of railroads economic development may be overestimated. To solve this problem, he used the statistics of the railway lines planned but never built during British colonial rule to conduct a placebo test, and found that these railway lines were not significantly correlated with agricultural incomes, which ruled out the possibility of the authority using economic growth potential as the basis for route and site selection.

2019 Nobel Laureate in Economics, Esther Duflo, and his collaborator Rohini Pande studied the economic development effects of large irrigation dams in India. Duflo and Pande (2007) analyzed agricultural production data of 271 regions in India from the year 1971 to 1999, and poverty data for 374 regions in the year 1973, 1983, 1987, 1993 and 1999. They found that river gradient affects a district's suitability for dams. In districts located downstream from a dam, agricultural production increases, and vulnerability to rainfall shocks declines. In contrast, agricultural production shows an insignificant increase in the district where the dam is located but its volatility increases. Similarly, rural poverty declines in downstream districts but increases in the district where the dam is built. This is mainly because in areas close to dams, where soil becomes saturated, the chances of rain-induced flooding are higher. In short, neither markets nor State institutions have alleviated the adverse distributional impacts of dam construction.

In his study targeting South Africa, Dinkelman (2011) investigated the employment effects of a mass roll-out of household electrification in rural South Africa using both instrumental variables and fixed effects. He found that female employment did indeed rise in response to new access to electricity in the home, and that this new infrastructure, while increasing the working hours of both men and women, lowered women's wages but increased men's. Further empirical evidence showed that the employment effects of electrification described above are primarily achieved by freeing women from home production.

In a study on Nigeria, Ogun (2010) used Nigeria's quarterly time series data from January 1970 to April 2005 and conducted the research based on a structural vector autoregressive (SVAR) model to analyze the poverty reduction effect of infrastructure. He found that infrastructure construction reduced poverty, while the effect of social infrastructure such as education and healthcare is greater than physical infrastructure projects such as transportation and communications.

In his study targeting Brazil, Lipscomb et al. (2013) estimated the development effects of electrification across Brazil over the period from 1960 to 2000. They first simulated a time series of hypothetical electricity grids for Brazil for the period 1960–2000 that show how the grid would have evolved had infrastructure investments been made based solely on geography-based cost considerations. Using the model as an instrument, they documented large positive effects of electrification on development that are underestimated when one fails to account for endogenous targeting. Through instrumental variable estimation, they found that the construction of hydropower plants improved the local Human Development Index (HDI), in terms of local life expectancy, education and income levels, increased the value of local properties, reduced poverty, and increased formal employment. Further research revealed that broad-based improvement in labor productivity across sectors and regions rather than general equilibrium re-sorting appears to be the likely mechanism by which these development gains are realized.

In a study on Argentina, Galiani et al. (2005) examined the impact of water system reforms on child mortality in Argentina. In the 1990s, about 30% of the cities in Argentina successively implemented the privatization reform of the water supply system. A difference-in-difference (DID) econometric model was designed according to the changes in the ownership of the water supply system in time and space. On average, water privatization reforms are estimated to reduce child mortality significantly, 8% higher in cities with water privatization reforms than in cities without reforms. For the poorest regions, the foregoing reduction ratio reached as high as 26%. Further research found that the privatization reforms reduced child mortality by reducing mortality from water sanitation-related diseases such as infectious and parasitic diseases.

3.2.2 Cross-Country Empirical Evidence

Devarajan et al. (1996) conducted a study using the panel data of 44 developing countries from 1970 to 1990. They found that an increase in the share of current expenditure has positive and statistically significant growth effects, while the relationship between the capital component of public expenditure (most of which is spent on infrastructure) and per-capita growth is negative. They believe that seemingly productive expenditures, when used in excess, could become unproductive. These results imply that developing-country governments have been misallocating public expenditures in favor of capital expenditures at the cost of current expenditures.

Strobl and Strobl (2011), following the footsteps of Duflo and Pande (2007), studied the distributional effects of large dams on farmland productivity of 59 drainage basins in 53 African countries. They used a hydrology-based spatial breakdown of the continent to exactly define regions in terms of their upstream/downstream relationship at a highly disaggregated level. Satellite data was also used to derive measures of cropland productivity within these areas. Through econometric analysis, they found that while regions downstream benefited from large dams, no beneficial effects accrued to cropland within the vicinity. At the same time, the productivity enhancing impact of upstream dams is dependent on the local climate. Overall, the research results suggest that upstream dams have quantitatively on average provided up to 12% of the minimum daily per capita amount of kilocalorie needs in downstream communities and raised agricultural production by 1%.

Pan et al. (2019) studied the positive impact of private provision of infrastructure on reducing poverty rates in developing countries based on data from 138 developing countries from 1996 to 2014. Through econometric analysis, they found that for every 1% increase in per-capita investment in infrastructure, the proportion of the population living on less than 3.10 US dollars per day in a country will decrease by 2.41%, while the proportion of the population living on less than 1.90 US dollars will drop by 1.55%. Another finding was that effective control of official corruption played a positive role in promoting private participation in infrastructure provision.

3.3 Effects of Infrastructure on China's Economic Development

The development effects of China's infrastructure have received widespread attention, mainly including their effects on economic growth, poverty reduction, and income distribution, as well as the internal mechanisms of how these effects happen.

3.3.1 Economic Growth Effects of Infrastructure

Liu and Hu (2010) studied the spillover effect of infrastructure on economic growth. Based on the panel data of 28 Chinese provinces (autonomous regions and municipalities) from 1988 to 2007, they systematically analyzed the relationship between the three major network infrastructure projects (transportation, energy, and information infrastructure) and TFP. They found that transportation infrastructure and information infrastructure had significant spillover effects on China's economic growth, while energy infrastructure produces less impact.

Zheng et al. (2014) studied the impact of telecommunications infrastructure on China's economic growth. Through econometric analysis using the panel data of 31 provinces (including autonomous regions and municipalities directly under the central government) from 1990 to 2010, they found that in the early stage, the construction of telecommunications infrastructure boosted economic growth, and when the technology reached maturity and after it peaked, its impact on economic growth became less positive. This research provides a basis for reshaping the development strategy for China's telecom infrastructure.

Some other scholars[2] have focused on the effects of transportation infrastructure. Zhang (2012) studied the spatial spillover effect of China's transportation infrastructure. By analyzing the provincial panel data from 1993 to 2009 using a spatial econometric model, he found that China's transportation infrastructure played an important role in China's regional economic growth, showing clear spatial spillover effects. The effects are predominantly positive, while there is also evidence of negative spatial spillover effects.

Zhou and Zheng (2012) studied the impact of the Beijing-Guangzhou Railway and the Beijing-Shanghai High-speed Railway on the economic growth of cities along the route. Based on the panel data of each city from the year 1994 to 2006, they divided cities into two groups: "cities affected by railway speed-up" and "cities not affected by railway speed-up", and then used the DID method to explore the causal effect of railway speed-up. They found that the speed-up promoted the economic growth of the stations along the route (measured by GDP growth per capita). Simultaneously, its impact on economic growth showed an incremental trend over time. This research reveals the positive impact of the improvement of transportation infrastructure quality on the economic growth of cities along the route.

Meanwhile, some studies have revealed the negative effect of excessive investment in infrastructure on economic growth. Sun et al. (2015) made an econometric analysis using China's provincial panel data from 2003 to 2012. They found that there is a significant inverted-U relationship between infrastructure construction investment and economic growth in the eastern and central China. Yet, a negative relationship can be found between infrastructure construction investment and economic growth in western China, which shows that infrastructure construction investment of high intensity may have an inhibitory effect on regional economic growth. Similarly, Liao et al. (2018) conducted econometric analysis using provincial panel data from 1993 to 2016. They found that infrastructure investment has a significant positive impact on China's economic growth on the whole, but this impact follows an obvious inverted U curve. This study reveals the fact that infrastructure investment has a weak effect on economic growth, which has implications for the formulation of development policies and structural adjustment of infrastructure investment.

[2] In recent years, research on the economic effects of China's high-speed rails has rapidly emerged, and Chapter 6 of this book focuses on reviewing papers studying these effects.

3.3.2 *Internal Mechanisms of the Economic Growth Effects of Infrastructure*

(1) Productivity

Some scholars have explored the internal mechanisms of how the economic growth effects of infrastructure happen from the perspective of productivity. Fan and Zhang (2004) explored the impact of rural infrastructure and other public capital on productivity in different regions. Using data from the China's 1996 Agricultural Census, they found that, overall, rural infrastructure and education could better interpret non-agricultural productivity. Meanwhile, the lower productivity in western China is mainly caused by the poor infrastructure, education, and technology in the rural areas of this region. Therefore, improving the scale and efficiency of public capital is one of the key tasks to narrow the productivity gap between western China and other regions.

Wan and Zhang (2017) distinguished and estimated the direct and indirect effects of infrastructure on productivity of enterprises, the latter being mainly derived from the agglomeration effects of infrastructure. By analyzing the micro-data of Chinese enterprises, they found that the three kinds of infrastructure (roads, communication servers, cables) can not only directly promote the productivity of enterprises, but also have a positive indirect impact on enterprise productivity through agglomeration effects.

(2) Market integration

Some scholars have studied the effects from the perspective of market integration. Liu and Hu (2011) studied the impact of transportation infrastructure on China's regional economic integration. Analyzing the data of inter-provincial freight volumes in 2008 through a gravity model, they found that the development of transportation infrastructure significantly boosted inter-provincial trade, which means that transportation infrastructure supports regional economic integration.

Fan et al. (2017) studied the impact of infrastructure construction on domestic market segmentation. By establishing a spatial Dubin Model to analyze the provincial panel data from 1993 to 2012, they found that the long-standing "beggar-thy-neighbor" phenomenon still exists in China. However, the direct effect of infrastructure construction is significant, which helps to optimize market segmentation. On the whole, however, the spatial spillover effect of infrastructure construction is not significant. Results of this research suggest that the government should not only strengthen the construction of cross-regional infrastructure, but also strengthen cross-provincial cooperation to achieve complementary advantages.

(3) Population agglomeration

Song and Li (2015) studied the relationship between infrastructure development and population agglomeration. Based on the panel data of 253 cities from 1997 to 2007, they examined the impact of 7 main railway lines and 6 railway speed-ups on the size of urban population during this period. They found that during the entire speed-up period, compared with cities without railway speed-up, the speed-up contributed to a 35.2% increase in the population of cities along the railway (i.e., cities with railway speed-up), which indicates that more labor flowed into cities with better transportation infrastructure, thus laying the foundation for economic growth.

3.3.3 Effects of Infrastructure on Poverty Reduction and Income Distribution

Liu et al. (2003) studied the impact of rural infrastructure investment on farmers' income and expenditure in poverty-stricken areas. They made an econometric analysis using the data of rural households in Guizhou from 1999 to 2000, and estimated the impact of investments in water provision, power grid, and roads on the income and expenditure of rural households in this province. They found that rural households in poverty-stricken areas benefited significantly from infrastructure investment. Meanwhile, the impact of infrastructure investment on rural households varies significantly depending on the possession of human capital, and those having more human capital benefit more from public investment. This research explains the poverty-reducing effect of infrastructure and the impact of human capital on this effect.

Guo and Gao (2009) studied the effect of China's infrastructure construction investment on poverty reduction. On the basis of reviewing China's poverty alleviation development strategy and the logic of poverty change, they conducted an econometric model analysis using China's rural infrastructure and poverty data from 1987 to 2006. They found that the development of China's poverty alleviation strategy changes with the connotation of the concept of poverty. The quantity and quality of infrastructure have important influences on reducing poverty and increasing farmers' income, and both should be paid attention to simultaneously. This study shows that improvement of infrastructure in quality and quantity have different impacts on rural households' income structure, which has implications for the design of policies and programs for poverty reduction in the rural areas.

Kang et al. (2014) studied the impact of the development of transportation infrastructure and the transportation industry on poverty reduction. They conducted an econometric analysis using panel data of transportation infrastructure and economic development of 30 Chinese provinces (including autonomous regions and municipalities directly under the central government) from 1998 to 2012. They found that roads and the road transportation industry can help narrow the urban–rural income gap, while railways and the rail transportation industry can narrow the urban–rural income gap and help reduce poverty only when their development reaches a certain level. The conclusion is that although transportation infrastructure plays a fundamental role in narrowing the urban–rural income gap, its role is conditional, with the level of railway development being a major determinant.

Liu et al. (2015) studied the effect of infrastructure on urban–rural income distribution. They conducted an econometric analysis using the panel data of urban–rural income gap, infrastructure, and labor transfer of 31 provinces (including autonomous regions and municipalities directly under the central government) from 1992 to 2010. They found that the improvement of transportation and communication infrastructure can bring about a significant improvement in income distribution, or narrow the urban–rural income gap. The improvement of infrastructure can significantly increase the income of rural households, while it has a significant positive impact on the income of urban residents. It can also promote the transfer of labor force from agriculture to non-agricultural sectors, thereby narrowing the urban–rural income gap. This research shows that improving infrastructure is an effective means to promote the transfer of agricultural labor force and a crucial material basis for promoting industrialization and urbanization.

Zhang and Wan (2016) examined the impact of rural infrastructure development on inclusive growth in China. Based on the China Health and Nutrition Survey, they used the landline telephone and tap water penetration rates to measure the level of infrastructure development. Through econometric analysis, they found that rural infrastructures such as landline telephones and tap water had helped raised the income level of rural households and close the urban–rural income gap in China, and lower-income households benefit more from rural infrastructure. This research shows the positive impact of infrastructure improvement in quantity and quality on income distribution, and has implications for improving urban–rural and regional income distribution.

3.4 Reflections on the Economic Growth Effects of China's Infrastructure

As literature survey reveals, the positive effects of infrastructure in promoting China's economic development have been repeatedly confirmed by empirical evidence, but there are also some studies that call attention to the problems and concerns arising from the effects of infrastructure on China's economic development.

First, infrastructure construction may help Chinese central cities attract factors of production and resources, resulting in the loss of resources on the part of small and medium-sized cities, and thus unbalanced development. Based on the concept of new economic geography, Faber (2014) dug into the fundamental issue of whether the construction of transportation infrastructure can reduce trade costs and whether trade cost reductions lead to the diffusion of industrial and total economic activity to peripheral regions, or do they reinforce the concentration of production in space? He regarded the construction of China's National Trunk Highway System (NTHS) as a large-scale natural experiment, and uses the "least-cost spanning tree" algorithm to construct a simulated highway network with the lowest construction cost. This highway was seen as an instrumental variable of the real highway network, thereby alleviating the problem of non-random selection of cities (nodes) connected by highways. The results of instrumental variable estimation show that highway network construction significantly reduces the economic growth rate of cities serving as nodes, especially the growth rate of industrial output. Faber believes that this is likely to be due to the reduction in trade costs between central cities and peripheral cities (i.e., nodes), making production more concentrated in central cities.

Second, barriers to labor mobility may hinder the realization of the positive effects of infrastructure. 2019 Nobel Laureates in Economics, Abhijit Banerjee, Esther Duflo and their collaborators studied the impact of transportation infrastructure accessibility on economic development of Chinese cities from the mid-1980s to early twenty-first century (Banerjee et al, 2020). They first constructed a straight-line network, connecting China's famous historical cities (Beijing, Chengdu, Guiyang, Kunming, Lanzhou, Nanchang, Taiyuan, and Xi'an) and treaty ports (Shanghai, Ningbo, Fuzhou, and Guangzhou) as the "historical traffic route" given exogenously. Then they measure the accessibility of the city's traffic infrastructure by the shortest distance from a city to the network, thus solving the endogenous problem of urban traffic infrastructure to a certain extent. Through econometric analysis, they found that proximity to transportation networks have a moderately sized positive causal effect on per capita GDP levels across sectors, but no effect on per capita GDP growth. They concluded that factor mobility plays an important role in determining the economic benefits of infrastructure development and the lack of factor mobility might limit the measured impact of better infrastructure.

Third, a debt-financed infrastructure investment may cause systematic financial risks in China. Ansar et al. (2016) systematically examined the impact and potential risks of China's infrastructure investment on economic development. They find that far from being an engine of economic growth, the typical infrastructure investment fails to deliver a positive risk adjusted return. More importantly, where investments are debt-financed, overinvesting in unproductive projects results in the buildup of debt, monetary expansion, instability in financial markets, and economic fragility. They conclude that China should shift to a lower level of higher-quality infrastructure investments as soon as possible to avoid an infrastructure-led financial and economic crisis.

Fourth, it must be pointed out that a country's governance system and governance capacity are the institutional basis for infrastructure to play a positive role. In previous research, the author has found that for developing countries, effective corruption control is a prerequisite for promoting private participation in infrastructure provision and reducing poverty (Pan and Wu 2019). The historical experience of developed countries also shows that government corruption is the fundamental cause for the lower quality of infrastructure (Glaser and Goldin 2012). These findings will be presented in subsequent chapters and further analyzed in Chap. 10.

References

Allen, R.C.: Global Economic History. Yilin Press, Translated by Lu Yun. Nanjing (2008)

Ansar, A., Fluvbjerg, B., Budzier, A.: Does infrastructure investment lead to economic growth or economic fragility? Evidence from China. Oxf. Rev. Econ. Policy **32**(3), 360–390 (2016)

Aschauer, D.A.: Is public expenditure productive? J. Monet. Econ. **23**(2), 177–200 (1989)

Banerjee, A., Duflo, E., Qian, N.: On the road: access to transportation infrastructure and economic growth in China. J. Dev. Econ. **145**, 102442 (2020)

Blaug, M.: Great Economics Before Keynes. Commercial Press, Translated by Feng Bingkun. Beijing (2015)

Coase, R.H.: The lighthouse in economics. J Law and Econom. **17**(2), 357–376 (1974)

Devarajan, S., Swaroop, V., Zou, H.F.: The composition of public expenditure and economic growth. J. Monet. Econ. **37**(2), 313–344 (1996)

Dinkelman, T.: The Effects of rural electrification on employment: new evidence from South Africa. Amer. Econom. Rev. **101**(7), 3078–3108 (2011)

Donaldson, D.: Railroads of the Raj: estimating the impact of transportation infrastructure. Amer. Econ Rev. **108**(4–5), 899–934 (2018)

Duflo, E., Pande, R.: Dams. Quart. J. Econ. **122**(2), 601–646 (2007)

Faber, B.: Trade integration, market size, and industrialization: evidence from China's national trunk highway system. Rev. Econ. Stud. **81**(3), 1046–1070 (2014)

Fan, S., Zhang, X.: Infrastructure and regional economic development in rural China. China Econ. Rev. **15**(2), 203–214 (2004)

Fan, X., Song, D., Zhao, X.: Has infrastructure construction broken domestic market segmentation? Econ. Res. **52**(2), 20–34 (2017)

Fogel, R.W.: Railroads and American Economic Growth: Essays in Econometric History. The Johns Hopkins University Press, Baltimore (1964)

Galiani, S., Gertler, P., Schargrodsky, E.: Water for life: the impact of the privatization of water services on child mortality. J. Polit. Econ. **113**(1), 83–120 (2005)

Glaeser, E.L., Goldin, C.: Corruption and Reform: Lessons from America's Economic History. Commercial Press, Translated by Hu Jiayong and Wang Zhaobin. Beijing (2012)

Guo, J., Gao, J.: Research on the poverty reduction effect of china's infrastructure construction investment: 1987–2006. Agricul. Econ. Issues **2009**(9), 63–71 (2009)

Hirschman, A.O.: The strategy of economic development. Economic Science Press, Translated by Cao Zhenghai and Pan Zhaodong. Beijing (1991)

Kang, J., Guo, M., Fu, Y.: To get rich, build roads first? An empirical study on transportation infrastructure construction, transportation industry development and poverty reduction. Explorat. Econom. Issues **2014**(9), 41–46 (2014)

Larsen, T.I., Pham, H.L. Rama, M.: the impact of infrastructure development on rural poverty reduction in Vietnam. World Bank Policy Research Working Paper, pp. 30790. (2004)

Liao, M., Xu, Z., Hu, C.: Can infrastructure investment promote economic growth? An empirical test based on provincial panel data from 1994 to 2016. Manage. World **2018**(5), 63–73 (2018)

Lipscomb, M., Mobarak, M.A., Barham, T.: Development effects of electrification: evidence from the topographic placement of hydropower plants in Brazil. Am. Econ. J. Appl. Econ. **5**(2), 200–231 (2013)

Liu, S., Hu, A.: Examination of infrastructure externalities in China: 1988–2007. Econ. Res. J. **45**(3), 4–15 (2010)

Liu, S., Hu, A.: Transportation infrastructure and china's regional economic integration. Econ. Res. **46**(3), 72–82 (2011)

Liu, X., Xin, X., Mao, X.: The impact of rural infrastructure investment in poor areas on farmer income and expenditure. China Rural Observ. **2003**(1), 31–36 (2003)

Liu, X., Zhang, X., Fang, W.: Urban-rural income distribution effect of infrastructure: from the perspective of labor transfer. World Econ. **38**(3), 145–170 (2015)

Marx, K.H. and Engels, F. Marx/Engels Collected Works.: Translated by Central Compilation and Translation Bureau for Works of Marx, Engels, Lenin and Stalin. Beijing, People's Press (1979)
Marx, K.H.: Das Capital, Volume I. Translated by Central Compilation and Translation Bureau for Works of Marx, Engels, Lenin and Stalin, Beijing, People's Press (2004)
Ogun, T.P.: Infrastructure and poverty reduction: implications for urban development in Nigeria. Urban Forum **21**(3), 249–266 (2010)
Pan, C., Wu, B.: Corruption control, private participation in infrastructure provision and its impact on poverty reduction: empirical evidence from developing countries (1996–2014). Southern Econ. **2019**(1), 60–80 (2019)
Roland, G.: Development Economics. Renmin University of China Press, Translated by Jin Zhinong. Beijing (2016)
Rostow, W.W.: The Stages of Economic Growth: A Non-communist Manifesto. China Social Sciences Press, Translated by Guo Xibao and Wang Songmao. Beijing (2001)
Samuelson, P.A.: The pure theory of public expenditure. Rev. Econ. Stat. **36**(4), 387–389 (1954)
Smith, A.: An Inquiry into the Nature and Causes of the Wealth of Nations. Commercial Press, Translated by Guo Dali and Wang Yanan. Beijing (2008)
Song, X., Li, K.: The impact of the improvement of transportation infrastructure quality on urban population size: an empirical analysis based on railway speed-up. Contemporary Econ. Sci. **37**(3), 19–26; 124–125 (2015)
Stiglitz, J.E., Rosengard, J.K.: Economics of the Public Sector, 4th edn. W. W. Norton & Company, New York (2015)
Strobl, E., Strobl, R.O.: The distributional impact of large dams: evidence from cropland productivity in Africa. J. Dev. Econ. **96**(2), 432–450 (2011)
Sui, F.: Innovation and Convergence: The American Revolution in New Economic History and Its Impact on China (1957–2004). Tianjin Ancient Works Publishing House, Tianjin (2009)
Sun, Z., Yang, G., Li, K.: Does infrastructure investment promote economic growth? Empirical evidence from East, Central and West. Economist **2015**(8), 71–79 (2015)
van de Walle, D.: Infrastructure and poverty in Vietnam. Living Standards Measurement Study Working Paper, pp. 121. (1996)
Wan, G., Zhang, Y.: The direct and indirect effects of infrastructure on corporate productivity: evidence from manufacturing in China. ADBI Working Paper, pp. 714. (2017)
Xi, J.: Speech at the Celebration of the 40th Anniversary of Reform and Opening-up. People's Publishing House, Beijing (2018)
Zhang, X.: Has China's transportation infrastructure promoted regional economic growth? And on the spatial Spillover effect of transportation infrastructure. Chinese Soc. Sci. **2012**(3), 60–77 (2012)
Zhang, X., Wan, G.: Does China's rural infrastructure promote inclusive growth? Econ. Res. **51**(10), 82–96 (2016)
Zheng, S., Zhou, L., He, W.: Telecommunication Infrastructure and China's economic growth. Econ. Res. **49**(5), 77–90 (2014)
Zhou, H., Zheng, X.: Quality of transportation infrastructure and economic growth: evidence from China's railway speed-up. World Econ. **35**(1), 78–97 (2012)

Chapter 4
A Review on Economic Models of Infrastructure

Once you start thinking about economic growth, it's hard to think about anything else.
—Robert Lucas, On the Mechanics of Economic Development

Abstract This chapter introduces four theoretical models of infrastructure economics and their policy implications, including the iceberg cost model, the endogenous growth model, the regional competition model, and another regional competition model that considers infrastructure's negative externalities.

This chapter introduces four theoretical models of infrastructure economics and their policy implications, including the iceberg cost model, the endogenous growth model, the regional competition model, and another regional competition model that considers infrastructure's negative externalities. This chapter is dedicated to revealing the impact of infrastructure on economic growth and the underlying mechanisms by analyzing the assumptions and equilibrium results of each model.

4.1 Iceberg Cost Model

The construction and improvement of railroads, roads and bridges can reduce transportation costs, thus promoting the development of inter-regional and international trade. This economic intuition forms the starting point for studying the economic effects of infrastructure. American economist Paul Samuelson has considered and made a mathematical analysis of the relationship between transportation costs and international trade (Samuelson 1964). In this section, Paul Samuelson's model is simplified to show the effects of infrastructure on trade more clearly.

Suppose there are two cities: city A and city B, and the prices of the same commodity (e.g., wheat) in city A and city B are P_A and P_B, respectively. The cost of transporting a unit of wheat from city A to city B is assumed to be a certain percentage

C. Pan, *Urban Infrastructure and Economic Development in China*, Public Economy and Urban Governance in China, https://doi.org/10.1007/978-981-99-6629-5_4

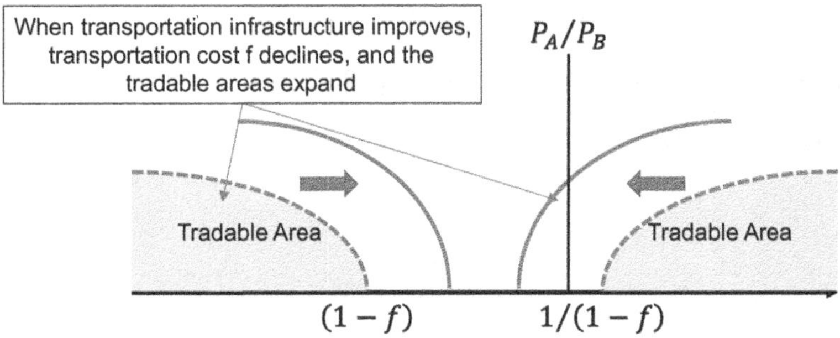

Fig. 4.1 Theoretical logic of infrastructure's effects on trade

f *(0% <* f *< 100%)* of the quantity. In other words, a portion of the commodity is lost or "evaporates" during transportation, hence the name "iceberg cost model".

Given $P_A < (1-f)P_B$, or $P_A/P_B < (1-f)$, it is profitable to transport wheat from city *A* to city *B*; but when $P_B < (1-f)P_A$, or $P_A/P_B > 1/(1-f)$, it is profitable to transport wheat from city *B* to city *A*. Therefore, when the inequality $(1-f) < P_A/P_B < 1/(1-f)$ holds true, city *A* and city *B* will not enter into wheat trade, constituting a non-tradable area $[(1-f), 1/(1-f)]$, and the higher the unit transportation cost f, the wider the non-tradable area, the smaller the probability of trade taking place. On the contrary, if the improvement of transportation infrastructure effectively reduces the unit transportation cost f, the smaller the non-tradable area, the higher the probability of trade.

Figure 4.1 illustrates the logic of infrastructure's effects on trade. In the initial state, P_A/P_B is within the non-tradable area of $[(1-f), 1/(1-f)]$ because there is not much price difference between city *A* and city *B*. When transportation infrastructure improves and the unit transportation cost f declines, the tradable areas on the left and the right expand simultaneously, and the relative price of wheat P_A/P_B between the two cities moves from the non-tradable area to the tradable area, thus generating trade activities between the two cities. In conclusion, the improvement of transportation infrastructure facilitates inter-regional trade by reducing transportation cost.

4.2 Endogenous Growth Model

The endogenous growth model, which has a long history, aims to prove that economic growth per capita exit or the growth of per capita output is greater than zero in a steady state or equilibrium. Scholars have found possible mechanisms for achieving endogenous growth through "learning by doing" and "knowledge spillovers". Robert J. Barro, a leading American macroeconomist, introduced public goods into the model of economic growth and discovered a new mechanism for achieving endogenous economic growth, which is called the "Barro Model". It is generally accepted that infrastructure projects such as transportation, communication, energy, and water infrastructure are obvious public goods, so this model can be used to reveal the link between infrastructure and economic growth.

4.2.1 Assumptions

Based on the research of Barro and Sala-i-Martin (2004), the following economic growth model can be developed. Suppose there are n firms in the economy and the i ($i = 1, 2, \ldots, n$) firm employs labor L_i and capital K_i. This economy's technical level is A and it has a productive infrastructure of size G. The infrastructure is non-competitive, i.e., the use of the infrastructure by any firm does not affect its use by other firms. Again assuming that the Cobb- Douglas production function applies to the firm, i.e., the production function of the *i-th* firm is

$$Y_i = AL_i^{1-\alpha}K_i^{\alpha}G^{1-\alpha} \tag{4.1}$$

In which α is the coefficient of capital output elasticity and satisfies $0 < \alpha < 1$. Based on this production function, four major conclusions can be drawn as follows.

First, infrastructure is noncompetitive, since G has no subscript i.

Second, given infrastructure size G, the scale reward of labor L and capital K remains constant.

Third, given labor L, the scale reward of infrastructure size G and capital K also remains constant.

Fourth, infrastructure size G can increase the marginal productivity of labor L and capital K (denoted as MPL and MPK), because

$$MPL = A(1-\alpha)L_i^{-\alpha}K_i^{\alpha}G^{1-\alpha} \tag{4.2}$$

$$MPK = A\alpha L_i^{1-\alpha}K_i^{\alpha-1}G^{1-\alpha} \tag{4.3}$$

This means that the infrastructure and the firm's input of production factors are complementary to each other.

Assuming further that the return on capital is r, the depreciation rate is δ, and the firm's objective to achieve maximum profit requires that the marginal productivity of capital aligns with the marginal cost, and that the average capital $k_i = K_i/L_i$, then:

$$MPK = A\alpha k_i^{\alpha-1}G^{1-\alpha} = r + \delta \tag{4.4}$$

Equation (4.4) implies that driven by the motive of profit maximization, firms choose the same level of capital per capita, i.e., $k_i = k$. Assuming that the total labor force in this economy is L, then the production function of each firm is:

$$Y = \sum\nolimits_{i=1}^{n} Y_i = \sum\nolimits_{i=1}^{n} AL_i k_i^{\alpha}G^{1-\alpha} = ALk^{\alpha}G^{1-\alpha} \tag{4.5}$$

Assuming that the output after consumption, capital depreciation and infrastructure provision in each period is used for capital accumulation, and revenues from one-time tax is used to finance the infrastructure provision, then:

$$\dot{K} = Y - C - \delta k - G \tag{4.6}$$

In which $\dot{K}$ is the growth rate of capital and C is consumption. Then, the dynamic equation of capital accumulation is

$$\dot{k} = Ak^{\alpha}G^{1-\alpha} - c - \delta k - G/L \tag{4.7}$$

In which c is the per capita consumption.

4.2.2 Model Setup and Solution

Assume that the social planner aims at maximizing consumer utility U over the entire period, so the following optimization model can be developed:

$$\max_{c,k,G} U = \int_{0}^{+\infty} e^{-\rho t} \cdot \frac{c^{1-\theta} - 1}{1-\theta} dt \tag{4.8}$$

$$subject\ to\ \dot{k} = Ak^{\alpha}G^{1-\alpha} - c - \delta k - G/L \tag{4.9}$$

In which t is time, $\dot{k}$ is growth of capital per capita, ρ is the discount factor and satisfies $0 < \rho < 1$, and the constant θ satisfies $\theta \geq 0$ and $\theta \neq 1$. Then, the Hamiltonian function is:

$$H = e^{-\rho t} \cdot \frac{c^{1-\theta} - 1}{1-\theta} + v(t) \cdot \left(Ak^{\alpha}G^{1-\alpha} - c - \delta k - G/L\right) \tag{4.10}$$

In which v is the transient utility. The first-order and transversality conditions are shown in Eqs. (4.11a), (4.11b) and (4.11c).

$$\begin{cases} \partial H/\partial c = e^{-\rho t}c^{-\theta} - v = 0 \\ \partial H/\partial G = A(1-\alpha)k^{\alpha}G^{-\alpha} - 1/L = 0 \\ \partial H/\partial k = v\left(A\alpha k^{\alpha-1}G^{1-\alpha} - \delta\right) = -\dot{v} \\ \lim\limits_{t\to+\infty} k(t) \cdot v(t) = 0 \end{cases} \tag{4.11a, b, c}$$

In which $\dot{v}$ is the growth rate of transient utility.

Through Eq. (4.11b), two major conclusions can be drawn:

First, $G = (1 - \alpha)Y$, or in equilibrium, infrastructure expands linearly along with economic growth. In other words, in equilibrium, infrastructure accounts for a fixed proportion of economic output $(1 - \alpha)$.

Second, $G = [A(1 - \alpha)L]^{1/\alpha}k$, i.e., in equilibrium, technological progress and population growth are positive factors that contribute to infrastructure expansion. In other words, in an economy with a higher level of technology and a larger population size, the scale of infrastructure is also larger.

By further organizing the above conditions and conclusions, we can obtain the dynamic equation of per capita consumption, which is

$$\dot{c}/c = (1/\theta)\left[\alpha A^{1/\alpha} \cdot (1 - \alpha)^{(1-\alpha)/\alpha} \cdot L^{(1-\alpha)/\alpha} - \delta - \rho\right] \tag{4.12}$$

In which $\dot{c}$ is the growth rate of per capita consumption. Equation (4.12) shows that in equilibrium the growth of per capita consumption is not zero, and an increase in population size L or in technology level A can increase the per capita consumption growth in equilibrium, which means endogenous economic growth is achieved.

In summary, the above model proves the possibility of endogenous economic growth by including infrastructure, a public good, into a standard model. Intuitively, it can be argued that any increase in population size can lower the tax burden per capita while people can enjoy the production effect of infrastructure because infrastructure is non-competitive, so per capita consumption goes up in equilibrium.

4.3 Regional Competition Model

Both the iceberg cost model and the endogenous growth model measure infrastructure's economic effects on the premise of a single economy and are therefore not applicable to scenarios where there are multiple regions. However, for a huge country like China and the United States, it is important to examine the distribution of infrastructure across regions within the country and the impact of infrastructure on development in each region, and its policy implications.

Cai and Treisman (2005) used the regional competition model to investigate the behavior of government investment in infrastructure with and without capital flows. This section provides a simplified model to highlight the impact of infrastructure on economic development in each region.

4.3.1 Assumptions

Suppose a country has n number of regions or local governments, and region i $(i = 1, 2, \ldots, n)$ can be expressed in the following Cobb–Douglas production function:

$$F_i = A_i k_i^{\alpha} I_i^{\beta} \tag{4.13}$$

In which $\alpha > 0, \beta > 0, \alpha + \beta < 1$. A_i is the innate endowment of region i, which can be interpreted as its governance capacity, geographical location, or human capital; I_i is local government investment in infrastructure, either economic infrastructure such as transportation and communication, or social infrastructure such as schools and hospitals, as long as it raises local output, and the investment in infrastructure is determined by the local government; and k_i is the size of the investor's capital invested in region I, assuming that total capital is a constant, i.e. $K = \sum_i k_i$.

Suppose the local government not only pursues local economic growth but also aims to increase its own consumption, i.e., the local government i has the following utility function:

$$U_i = (1 - t_i)F_i + \theta c_i \tag{4.14}$$

In which t_i is the macro tax rate of region i; c_i is the government consumption in region i; and $\theta(\theta > 0)$ measures the relative preference of the government of region i between after-tax output and its own consumption. The above assumptions imply that the local government is neither a selfless "charitable organization" that exclusively seeks to maximize output, nor a profit-oriented Leviathan that aims to maximize its own consumption; it is an institution with a partial self-interest orientation. Obviously, this assumption is compatible with reality.

Further assume that a local government has financial resources R at the beginning, and the macro tax rate is consistent across regions, i.e., $t_i = t > 0(\forall i)$. The local government spends its initial financial resources R and tax revenues tF_i on infrastructure provision and its own consumption. Based on this, the budget constraint equation for local government i can be obtained:

$$I_i + c_i = R + tF_i \tag{4.15}$$

4.3.2 Model Setup and Solution

Assume that the game between local governments and investors is like this: first, each local government determines both its infrastructure investment and its own consumption, and then the investor decides the scale of the investment in each region. Given that capital can move freely across regions, capital will inevitably flow from regions with lower after-tax marginal productivity of capital to regions with higher marginal productivity of capital until the after-tax return on capital is exactly the same across regions. Due to the large number of regions, no region can affect the after-tax return on capital, but can only accept it. For this reason, the nationwide after-tax return on capital can be set to r.

If the infrastructure investment of local government i is I_i, and investors decide the scale of investment in each region based on this, then:

$$r = (1 - t) \cdot \partial F_i / \partial k_i \tag{4.16}$$

Taking the regional production function into consideration, the optimal response function of capital investment in region i is:

$$\tilde{k}_i(I_i) = \left[\frac{1}{r}(1 - t)\alpha A_i I_i^{\beta}\right]^{1/(1-\alpha)} \tag{4.17}$$

As Eq. (4.17) shows: first, the more infrastructure investment is made in a region, the more investment would be attracted, which is the "regional competition effect"; second, the better a region's natural endowment is, the more capital it can attract, meaning that factors that are unlikely to change in the short run, such as governance capacity, geographic location, and human capital, are often the key drivers behind regional disparities, which is the "endowment effect".

Following the principle of backward induction, the local government will base its decision on the optimal response of investors. The optimization problem for local government i is:

$$\max_{I_i, c_i} U_i = (1 - t) F_i\left(\tilde{k}_i, I_i\right) + \theta c_i \tag{4.18}$$

$$subject\ to\ I_i + c_i = R + t F_i\left(\tilde{k}_i, I_i\right) \tag{4.19}$$

After substituting budget constraint into the utility function and eliminating the government consumption c_i, the above problem is transformed into an unconstrained optimization problem. Given the existence of an interior solution, the first order condition is derived:

$$\frac{\partial F_i}{\partial \tilde{k}_i}\frac{\partial \tilde{k}_i}{\partial I_i} + \frac{\partial F_i}{\partial I_i} = \frac{\theta}{1 + (\theta - 1)t} \tag{4.20}$$

Which leads to

$$I_i^* = \rho_1(\alpha, \beta, \theta, r, t) \cdot A_i^{1/(1-\alpha-\beta)} \tag{4.21}$$

Substituting I_i^* into the investor's optimal response function yields

$$k_i^* = \rho_2(\alpha, \beta, \theta, r, t) \cdot I_i^* \tag{4.22}$$

In which ρ_1, ρ_2 are functions of the constants. If we classify the natural endowments of a region into two categories, namely $A_B, A_P (A_B > A_P)$, then we have

$$\frac{I_B^*}{I_P^*} = \frac{k_B^*}{k_P^*} = \left(\frac{A_B}{A_P}\right)^{1/(1-\alpha-\beta)} \tag{4.23}$$

Equation (4.23) shows that the disparity of regional natural endowments widens the gap of infrastructure investment by different local governments, which in turn expands the disparity of capital investment in each region, which is the "Matthew effect" ("for unto every one that hath shall be given, and he shall have abundance: but from him that hath not shall be taken away even that which he hath").

This means that under regional capital competition, local governments' investment in infrastructure magnifies the effect of regional natural endowments, thus widening the development gap between regions. Local governments of regions with strong governance, good geographic location, and abundant human capital tend to invest more heavily in infrastructure, which attracts capital inflows and drives economic growth. For instance, cities in the Yangtze River Delta have better infrastructure and a more friendly business environment, so foreign investment pours in steadily. On the contrary, in regions with weak governance and suffering from geographic isolation and human capital shortages, the local governments lack incentives to invest in infrastructure and do not expect capital inflows, but focus on government consumption. As in some poor central and western regions of China, the local governments are unwilling to invest in infrastructure to attract investment; instead, they prefer to seek financial transfers from the central government to maintain local socioeconomic operations.

In conclusion, this model not only theoretically reveals how infrastructure influences local capital competition, which widens the regional development gap, but also explains the differences between local governments concerning investment in infrastructure and government consumption, so it has high theoretical and practical relevance.

References

Cai, H.B., Treisman, D.: Does competition for capital discipline governments? Decentralization, globalization and public policy. Amer. Econ. Rev. **95**(3), 817–830 (2005)

Samuelson, P.A.: Theoretical notes on trade problems. Rev. Econ. Statist. **46**(2), 145–154 (1964)

Chapter 5
Achievements and Challenges of Infrastructure Development in China Over the Past 70 Years

The mountain goddess if she is still there
will marvel at a world so changed.
—Mao Zedong, "Prelude to Water Melody: Swimming"

This chapter divides the 70 years from the founding of the People's Republic of China in 1949 to 2019 into two phases, one before and the other after the launch of reform and opening-up in 1978, reviews China's achievements in infrastructure development and its major initiatives and policies concerning infrastructure, and discusses the model, laws, strengths, and weaknesses of China's infrastructure development through an economic analysis.

5.1 China's Infrastructure Development During Socialist Economic Reconstruction (1949–1978)

Since 1949, China has made great social and economic accomplishments through trial and error. "Today, a socialist China is standing firm in the East. No force can ever undermine our great motherland's status, or stop the Chinese people and the Chinese nation from marching forward" (Xi 2019).

Over the past 70 years, China's infrastructure, ranging from transportation, communications, energy to water facilities, has grown phenomenally and become a fundamental force behind its national economic and social development. As Chinese President Xi Jinping said, "China has made remarkable achievements in infrastructure development. Now, we boast smooth information flows, a complete and easily accessible network of crisscrossing roads, expressways, and high-speed rails, high dams, West–East gas transmission pipelines, and South-to-North water transfer routes. Now, with so many vehicles, ships and planes coming and going, traveling in, to and from China has become very easy" (Xi 2018). China's infrastructure development is beyond doubt a miracle. Facing the new era, it is necessary to anticipate the challenges China may face in the future based on reviewing its experience in infrastructure development.

C. Pan, *Urban Infrastructure and Economic Development in China*, Public Economy and Urban Governance in China, https://doi.org/10.1007/978-981-99-6629-5_5

Fig. 5.1 Two periods of China's history since 1949.

To better understand China's infrastructure development, this chapter divides the past 70 years into two periods: the period of socialist economic reconstruction (from the founding of People's Republic of China in 1949 to the launch of reform and opening-up in 1978); and the period of reform and opening-up (from 1978 to the 70th anniversary of the founding of the People's Republic of China in 2019) (see Fig. 5.1). First, this chapter presents China's general achievements in key areas in each period, then describes the historical background of each period and analyzes the reform initiatives, and development achievements in each period, and finally, based on historical review, explores the fundamental law of China's infrastructural development through an economic analysis.

5.1.1 Reparation and Construction of Infrastructure During Economic Recovery (1949–1952)

In the first years, China's transportation infrastructure, including railways, roads, ports, and waterways, was almost in ruins after decades of war and had to be rebuilt. In 1949, China's total railway mileage was only 22,000 km, lower than the total of Britain in 1880, and to make it worse: 41% of its railways were located in Northeastern China, while east–west trunk rails in Central China were lacking, and the northwestern and southwestern regions had so few railways that they were isolated and economic connections were cut off (Wu and Dong 2010). At that time, roads ran a total of 149,000 km in China, but less than 60% was usable and only 39% was paved, severely limiting land transportation. On the side of ports and waterways, many ports were in disrepair and waterways were blocked. Among them, Tianjin Port, the largest port in North China, was so damaged that it was not working. In brief, China's war-ravaged infrastructure posed a serious restriction on its economic recovery and development.

This forced the government to give priority to infrastructure development. As Chen Yun, one of the pioneers and founders of China's socialist economic system, pointed out, "To restore and further develop our secondary sector, we must create some favorable conditions. The first task is to restore transportation, especially rail transportation" (Liu 2009). He stressed that "transportation is the engine of national economy" and proposed to make urgent repairs on the major projects first and build more later.

In 1949, the Ministry of Railways was established under the Chinese People's Revolutionary Military Commission to coordinate reconstruction and management of railways across the country. Thanks to the hard work of the Ministry of Railways, as well as railway engineers, remobilized military troops and the general public, the existing railways of over 8000 km were restored within a year. On January 2, 1950, Xinhua News Agency declared that "the nationwide network of railways has been basically restored, which will closely connect the capital city Beijing with other major cities, link up the front and the hinterland, and build inter-connectivity between cities along the railways with the vast rural areas, factories, and mines. It will also help the People's Liberation Army liberate Tibet and Hainan Island, and play a positive role in developing the national economy" (Chen 2009).

Meanwhile, the construction of new railways began soon. By the end of 1952, 1,473 km of new railways were completed. Among them, the Laibin-Munanguan Line in Guangxi (Southwestern China), the Chengdu-Chongqing Line in Sichuan (Southwestern China), and the Tianshui-Lanzhou Line in Gansu (Northwestern China) were completed and opened to traffic in October 1951, July 1952, and October 1952.

Both the restored and newly built railway lines increased the capacity of China's rail transportation: from 1950 to 1952, the total throughput of railways rose by 31.48%, in which freight throughput was up 54%. In short, the construction of railways was a key factor in recovering and stabilizing China, economically and politically, in the first years after liberation (1949).

With respect to roads and waterways, the Ministry of Transport was established at the First Plenary Session of the Chinese People's Political Consultative Conference on the eve of the founding of the People's Republic of China in 1949, with the mandate to promote water and road transportation nationwide.

In 1950, the Government Administration Council (later transformed into the State Council) of the Central Government issued the *Decision on Road Transportation Tasks in 1950*. According to this Decision, local governments were required to mobilize forces to repair the existing roads and highways, refurbish road vehicles, and improve the capacity of transportation; and private investment was encouraged under the leadership of State-owned Enterprises to advance public–private cooperation on road transportation. In the same year, the Ministry of Transport proposed that new roads should be built in a well-planned way while repairing the existing roads. With the joint efforts of remobilized military troops, road workers and the general public, the construction of roads proceeded rapidly throughout the country. By the end of

1952, the mileage of roads had gone up to 130,000 km, and a total of 303 major lines had completed urgent repair, reconstruction, restoration, or construction.

Regarding water transportation, the Government Administration Council issued the *Decision on Waterway Tasks in 1950*, which aimed to promote inland navigation and port development since 1950. Since then, the government has systematically carried out tasks such as dredging harbors and rivers, restoring wharf warehouses, and salvaging and repairing ships. The government also supported the development of private shipping agencies, as part of its efforts to recover the national economy. Port restoration was carried out immediately. In a time when construction machines and professionals were in extreme shortage, it took only about one year to restore the Port of Tanggu, which was officially opened in October 1952 and quickly became the international trade and shipping hub of Northern China. From 1949 to 1952, the restoration of waterways across the country made remarkable progress: 17.36 million and 11.87 million cubic meters of mud were dredged from ports and river courses, and the capacity of water transportation scored a rapid annual growth of 26.4%. The recovery of water transportation effectively made up for the shortfall in rail and road transportation.

In air transportation, the Civil Aviation Administration was established under the People's Revolutionary Military Commission in 1949. From 1950 to 1952, the total length of air routes increased from 12,131 to 13,885 km, and air cargo throughput rose from 104.3 tons to 108.4 tons.

In posts and telecommunications, the Ministry of Posts and Telecommunications was established in 1949. From 1950 to 1952, the capacity of long-distance telecommunications increased by 115.61%, the capacity of local telephone exchanges increased by 106.96%, and the total length of postal routes extended from 863,000 km to 1.29 million kilometers.

In terms of water conservancy and irrigation facilities, the Ministry of Water Resources was established in 1949. The ministry mobilized efforts to improve water conservancy and farmland irrigation, working on a host of major projects including the Huaihe River rehabilitation project, embankment, and rehabilitation projects in the lower reaches of the Yellow River, the Jingjiang River flood diversion and control project and the rehabilitation of the Yi River and the Shu River, and completing some major projects soon including the Guanting Reservoir, the Foziling Reservoir, and the Sanhe Gate. The development of water infrastructure has prevented rivers from harming people's life and assets and created farming benefits, helping recover and develop the national economy.

To sum up, from 1949 to 1952, the Chinese government followed the principle of New-democratic Economy[1] in the reconstruction of the national economy. When financial resources were not yet abundant enough to support the massive construction of infrastructure, the government mobilized various non-government forces to participate in the construction of infrastructure, and succeeded in repairing and building a

[1] "New-democratic Economy" refers to the transitional or mixed economy led by the State economy of socialist nature before China really entered socialism. It consisted of various economic components such as the State, cooperatives, individual businesses, and private capitalism.

large amount of infrastructure. These efforts had proved their value in the recovery of national economy.

5.1.2 Development of Infrastructure During Transition to Socialism (1953–1956)

Around 1953, China and the world underwent profound changes: domestically, national economy recovered and land reform was basically completed, while outside China, the war to resist US aggressors and aid Korea (the Korean War) was coming to an end, but the economic blockade imposed by the West was still tight. In the hope of achieving prosperity and based on an assessment of the international political situation, Chairman Mao Zedong delivered an important speech at the expanded meeting of the Political Bureau of the Central Committee on June 15, 1953, pointing out that "the Party's overarching task for this transitional period is to basically industrialize the country and complete the shift towards socialism in agriculture, the individual craft sector, and capitalist industry and commerce within ten to fifteen years or more. This will be our general guideline that direct our efforts and activities. We must hold fast to this guideline, or we will make left or right-leaning mistakes."

Following this guideline, China formulated the First Five-Year Plan for the development of the national economy from 1953 to 1957. The main task of the First Five-Year Plan was to pool and mobilize resources to advance the industrial development program that was designed with the help of the Soviet Union and consisted of 694 large and medium-sized projects with a special focus on 156 key projects in order to pave the ground for China's socialist industrialization and ensure the steady growth of the share of socialist elements in the national economy.

Most of the key 156 projects under the First Five-Year Plan, designed and implemented with the help of the Soviet Union, were in heavy industries: 150 projects had been carried out, including 44 in the defense industry, 20 in the metallurgical industry, 52 in the energy industry, 24 in the machinery industry, and 10 in the chemical industry and light industry (Yuan 2019), and capital investment in heavy industries amounted to 85% of total industrial investments. In this sense, the First Five-Year Plan strategically prioritized the development of heavy industries. However, heavy industry projects, which have long latency periods between initiation and completion, depended on imported technologies and equipment and required huge investments, so they were big challenges given China's resource endowment, low capital accumulation, low foreign exchange reserves, and limited capital mobilization at that time. It was unrealistic to achieve the rapid development of heavy industries by utilizing market access to obtain resources (Lin et al. 2002).

In this context, in order to achieve its strategic goals, it was essential for the government to intervene in market pricing and resource allocation through official planning. First, the government suppressed the prices of agricultural products, raw materials, wages, and foreign exchange rates to reduce the cost of building heavy industries;

second, the government channeled resources through official allocation to the industrial sector, especially heavy industries; and finally, in order to prevent businesses from deviating from State objectives, the government implemented the "socialist transformation" of the means of production in agriculture, individual craft industry and capitalist industry and commerce, which means nationalizing the producing enterprises and thus depriving them of the right to make autonomous decisions on production and operation. At the same time, the government strengthened infrastructure construction to support the development of national economy, especially heavy industries.

The above policies and measures, which were mutually enhancing, all focused on the development of heavy industries. As a result, the country registered great achievements in economic development during the First Five-Year Plan period: by the end of 1957, all targets of the First Five-Year Plan were completed, and the national economy took on a new look; in 1957, the total output value of agriculture and industry came to 124.1 billion RMB yuan, up 67.8% from the 1952 level, in which the total output value of industry reached 70.4 billion RMB yuan, up 128.6% from 1952; and by the end of 1957, 135 of the 156 key projects had started, and 68 of them had been fully or partially completed and put into operation.

During the First Five-Year Plan period, transportation and other infrastructure projects developed by leaps and bounds, too. The First Five-Year Plan proposed to "develop transportation, light industries, agriculture, and commerce where appropriate". By the end of 1957, the mileage of railroads reached 29,862 km, up 22% from the 1952 level. Over these five years, 33 new railroads were built and 3 were restored. The Baoji-Chengdu Railway, the first bridge over the Yangtze River in Wuhan, and the Yingtan-Xiamen Railway were completed and opened to traffic in 1956, 1957, and 1958. By the end of 1957, the mileage of highways in China came to 250,000 km, up 100% from 1952. The Qinghai-Tibet Highway and the Ya'an-Tibet Highway were completed and opened to traffic in 1954. Beijing Capital International Airport (BCIA), the first civilian airport of China, began construction in 1955 and was put into operation in 1958. The Yumen Oilfield was basically completed in 1957. No doubt, the steady improvement of infrastructure had provided a strong support for developing heavy industries and played a role in realizing China's strategic goals.

5.1.3 Development of Infrastructure While Exploring the Path of Socialism (1957–1978)

During the First Five-Year Plan period, China's national economy developed rapidly and the industrial system took shape and gained scale. Based on these achievements, China continued to focus on its heavy industries. In 1956, the Second Five-Year Plan (1958–1962) began, and the main tasks were to "continue the industrial development centered on heavy industries, promote technological transformation to drive the national economy, and lay a solid foundation for socialist industrialization in

China." The Plan also included specific growth objectives: in 1962, the total output value of industry and agriculture should increase by about 75% over the level of 1957, in which the total output value of industry should roughly double.

However, centralized planning had some inherent drawbacks which emerged soon. Due to the massive scale of national economy and the wide variety of local conditions, it became increasingly difficult for the central government to formulate targeted plans and monitor their implementation. There were many cases of "plans lagging behind changes in reality". In short, the inherent information asymmetry between the central government and local governments strained the centralized planning system and restricted the initiative of local governments to develop economy. Commenting on the relationship between the central government and local governments in the article "On the Ten Major Relationships" published in 1956, Chairman Mao Zedong emphasized that "local governments should be empowered and given more autonomy while the central government effectively plays its leadership role in maintaining national unity and coordination."

Against this backdrop, China implemented its first economic reform in 1958, which was a tentative move of decentralization. The central government delegated to local governments some of its powers in planning, enterprise governance, material distribution, project approval, fiscal budget and taxation, and labor management, but the basic economic system and the resource allocation method were maintained. In the academia, this reform was described as "institutional power division" or "administrative decentralization", which maintains the centralized planning model while decentralizing some planning powers to local governments. It was not an attempt of "decentralization through market", or giving autonomous power to enterprises through market-oriented reforms (Wu 2004). However, this "institutional power division" finally led to disruptions in the national economy, causing inefficient uses of scarce resources and a steady decline in economic efficiency. After 1959, the country suffered from severe economic woes.

Facing this plight, in 1960, the CPC Central Committee proposed a dramatic remedy, including measures to adjust the economic structure, consolidate its development gains, raise production capability, and make across-the-board improvements in order to alleviate the economic burdens and troubles caused by the "Great Leap Forward" movement. The CPC Central Committee also decided to spend three years (1963–1965) as an adjustment or transitional period to create conditions for the implementation of the Third Five-Year Plan (1966–1970). During this adjustment phase, most of the planning powers delegated to local governments in 1958 returned to the hands of the central government, centralized planning was reinstated, iron and steel facilities falling below production standards were abandoned, and rural workers who had been temporarily summoned were sent back. This dramatic change brought the national economy back on track very soon, and by 1963 the national economy had stabilized and begun to recover.

The re-centralization of planning powers eased the division between local governments, basically restored collaboration among local governments and the relationship between upstream and downstream links of supply chains, and resolved the contradiction between material shortage and surging demand. As the national economy recovered, local governments played more independent and proactive roles in economy development, and they were given the power to manage capital investments in many non-industrial areas, develop targets for locally managed enterprises and institutions, and allocate incomes from small coal mines, refineries, cement plants, glassworks, and thermal power plants (Hu 2001).

At the same time, China continued to strategically prioritize the development of heavy industries and the national defense industry, ambitiously wanting to catch up with and even overtake the world's advanced levels. In 1964, the Third Five-Year Plan was issued with the emphasis put on developing manufacturing industry while guaranteeing agricultural production and national defense. The annual average growth target for the five years was 7%. At the same time, considering the international situation, China began to implement the Third-front Movement (moving production facilities to the hinterland), a major strategic decision that gradually moved China's industrial production from east to west (particularly the southwest and the northwest).

The main objectives of the Third Five-Year Plan were achieved thanks to the accumulation during the three-year transitional period and the practicability of the Plan, despite disruptions by the Cultural Revolution. Over these five years, China's national economy grew by an annual average of 9.95%, and the total output value of agriculture and industry grew by 9.6% annually, in which the annual average growth of the total output value of agriculture came to 3.9% and that of industry came to 11.7%. China's infrastructure also witnessed a rapid development: in 1967, the first generator of the Qingtongxia Hydropower Station went into operation; in 1970, Dongfanghong I China's first man-made satellite was successfully launched; and in the same year, the Chengdu-Kunming Railway was completed and put into operation. All these indicated that the Third Five-Year Plan initially created an independent and relatively complete industrial system and national economic system.

These achievements of economic development, however, could not cover up the shortcomings of the centralized planning system. In 1970, under the framework of planned economy, the State once again pushed for an economic system reform centered on administrative decentralization, delegating the administrative power over most enterprises and institutions directly under central government ministries to local managements. Within a very short time, over 2,600 enterprises, institutions, and construction companies directly under the central government were handed over to their respective provinces, municipalities, and autonomous regions. This reform, following the same logic as the decentralization move in 1958, once again disrupted inter-regional collaboration and economic ties between upstream and downstream enterprises and industries, disrupting the production of enterprises and reducing economic efficiency. Facing the chaos, the government again implemented a series of remedy measures to strengthen unified planning and improve enterprise operation. However, decimated by the Cultural Revolution, China's economic efficiency kept declining and the national economy came to the verge of collapse.

During the Fourth Five-Year Plan period (1971–1975), despite economic hardships and disruptive political movements, China's national economy made remarkable achievements: the national economy grew by an annual average of 7.76%, and the total output value of agriculture and industry grew by an annual average of 7.8%, in which the total output value of agriculture was up 4.0% annually and the total output value of industry was up 9.1%. At the same time, China made breakthroughs in the construction of railroads, water infrastructure, oil exploration, satellite launch and recovery, and computer research and development. In 1973, China's first integrated-circuit electronic computer capable of one million operations per second ran a successful trial in Beijing; in 1974, Dagang Oilfield and Shengli Oilfield were built; in the same year, the Hunan-Guizhou Railway was completed and opened to traffic; in 1975, Liujiaxia Hydropower Station, then the largest hydropower project of China, was completed; and in the same year, China launched a recoverable remote-sensing satellite and successfully recovered it, becoming the third country to master the satellite recovery technology after the United States and the Soviet Union. No doubt, these are great achievements made by the Party and the people regardless of the Cultural Revolution.

5.2 Leapfrog Infrastructure Development During Reform and Opening-Up (1978–2019)

5.2.1 Infrastructure Development in the Early Years of Reform and Opening-Up (1978–1984)

In December 1978, the 3rd Plenary Session of the 11th Central Committee of the CPC was held, which realized a major turn of far-reaching significance in the history of the Party since the founding of the People's Republic of China and embarked on the great journey of reform, opening-up, and socialist modernization (Xi 2018). Since then, the priority of the CPC and the government has shifted to socialist modernization, and reform and opening-up has become the megatrend of China's development.

In the early years of reform and opening-up, China did not follow the previous approach of administrative decentralization for its economic transformation, but focused on expanding enterprise autonomy. In 1979, the State Council issued the *Regulations on Expanding the Autonomy of State-Owned Industrial Enterprises*, which gave administrative and operational rights to enterprises. Although this move motivated the enterprise sector and created unprecedented enthusiasm for production and investment, the lack of an effective mechanism to respond to and handle the relationship between material supply and demand made enterprises hungry for investment again, driving up monetary wages and fiscal deficits, and pulling back the national economy into disorder.

Meanwhile, non-State economic forces have grown up amid the unfriendly circumstances, which injected a new impetus into China's economic development.

Since 1980, the household responsibility system had been widely implemented in rural areas, greatly improving agricultural productivity, and sparing a large amount of labor for the development of industry in the coastal urban areas. During those years, enterprises owned by towns and townships, mainly collectively owned, sprang up across the country. Since 1983, private enterprises had also developed rapidly. Opening its door to the global, China set up four Special Economic Zones in Shenzhen, Zhuhai, Shantou, and Xiamen in 1980, and later opened 14 coastal cities in 1984, which gave a strong boost to processing trade and foreign investment. In 1985, the non-State economic entities, including collective, private, and foreign-funded enterprises, accounted for over 35% of China's total industrial output value, and this share rose to over 45% in 1990 (Wu 2004). In this way, the non-State economic sector gradually became an important part of the national economy.

In October 1984, the 3rd Plenary Session of the 12th Central Committee of the CPC was held, which reviewed and adopted the *Decision of the Central Committee of the Communist Party of China on the Reform of Economic Structure*. According to this document, China decided to shift the focus of economic reform from rural to urban areas and shift towards a socialist commodity economy, and emphasized that a reasonable price system is essential to the economic structure reform. That means China took a firm step towards a market economy system.

A review of the reform measures of the early 1980s shows that China did not directly employ the shock therapy of abolishing the planned economy and changing the ownership of state-owned enterprises abruptly. Instead, China kept the basic framework of planned economy and the state-owned sector, but at the same time cultivated new economic forces from outside the State-owned sector, the growth of which created good conditions for later reforms in the State-owned sector. These pilot reforms were referred to by some scholars as "incremental reforms", as opposed to systemic reforms.

During the Sixth Five-Year Plan period (1981–1985), China continued to adjust its economic structure, consolidate its development gains, raise production capability, and make across-the-board improvements, an initiative that began in the transitional phase. Meanwhile, China actively adjusted the proportion of the national economy and achieved rapid growth. During these five years, China's GDP increased by an average of 10.72% per year, in which the total agricultural output rose by an average of 10.8% per year, and the total industrial output value rose by 10.6% annually. On the side of infrastructure development, drawing on lessons learned during the Fifth Five-Year Plan (1976–1980) when the scale of capital investments was too large, the latency period was too long, and investments were not effective, China reduced the scale of large and medium-sized projects and focused on energy and transportation projects, including water resources and hydraulic power projects in the upper reaches of the Yellow River, the middle and upper reaches of the Yangtze River and the Red River basin, as well as pithead power stations and thermal power plants in areas with rich coal resources and areas with high electricity consumption. From 1981 to 1985, China built 2000 km of new railroads, added a track to 1700 km of railroads, and electrified 2500 km of railroads. In 1984, the first phase of the Qinghai-Tibet Railway was completed and opened to traffic; and in the same year, the

Dongfanghong II experimental communication satellite was successfully launched. These were landmarks of China's infrastructure development during the Sixth Five-Year Plan period.

5.2.2 Infrastructure Development While China Explored Socialist Market Economy (1985–1993)

After the mid-1980s, as a result of the "incremental reforms" and the growth of the non-State economy, China's national economy developed in such a way that State and non-State sectors coexisted and hence two pricing mechanisms coexisted for the same commodity or means of production. In other words, State-owned enterprises could obtain "planned" production materials at lower state prices and purchase the excess at higher market prices, while non-State enterprises had to purchase all production materials at market prices. In 1985, the *Notice on Liberalizing Prices for Surplus Outputs from Industrial Production* was issued, allowing enterprises to sell and purchase "unplanned" materials at market prices, which marked the official recognition of a double-track pricing model.

The existence of dual pricing rules, the inevitable result of China's incremental economic reforms, played a positive role in the survival and growth of the non-State sector. Although the non-State sector bore higher production costs than the Sate-owned sector and was less competitive, the dual-track pricing model had, after all, created "a crack in the iron wall" of the planned economy for market entities and provided a narrow space for skilled craftsmen to run their own business. At the same time, the dual-track pricing model did not affect the vested interests of the State-owned sector, thus reducing their resistance to future reforms.

However, it must be noted that, as a temporary pricing arrangement during the transitional period, this dual-track pricing model was by no means a lasting solution. A discriminatory pricing model like this would not only undermine the efficiency of resource allocation, but also hinder the private economy from further development. In their paper "The Transition to a Market Economy: Pitfalls of Partial Reform" published in 1992, three American economists used a simple model to estimate the consequences of implementing a partial reform (i.e., a dual-track pricing model) on welfare, showing that this dual-track approach would unexpectedly result in a substantial diversion of subsidized inputs away from the State firms and toward private firms even when State firms value these inputs more (Murphy et al. 1992). They noted that, unlike the Soviet Union's comprehensive dual-track pricing model, Chinese firms were only allowed to sell "unplanned" materials at market prices, which guaranteed the supply of means of production to the State-owned sector. Thus, the welfare loss resulting from China's dual-track pricing model was smaller.

Worse yet, the dual-track pricing model had resulted in market speculation that had negative economic effects. Some people bribed government officials in order to obtain "planned" materials, and then sell them at market prices to gain huge profits. This corrupt practice had aroused strong protests from all sectors of society.

To cope with this problem, the government tried to unify the pricing mechanisms fast, but failed. The "1988 Price Reform" triggered a widespread fear of rapid inflation, causing a nationwide bank run and panic buying. This failed attempt endangered the national economy, and was urgently revoked (Xiao 2019). After that, China mainly worked on regulating the economic environment and restoring the economic order, and shifted the focus to the "management contract system" of State-owned enterprises.

In the early 1990s, there were heated debates on the ongoing market-oriented reform. As many people doubted the effectiveness of the market, the prospects of the reform were unclear for a while. At this critical moment, Deng Xiaoping, the chief architect of reform and opening-up, took a month-long "Southern tour" to Wuchang, Shenzhen, Zhuhai, and Shanghai from January to February 1992, and delivered a series of talks, known as "Deng Xiaoping's Southern Tour Talks" which cleared up confusions concerning the market-oriented reform. He once said, "The proportion of planning to market forces is not the essential difference between socialism and capitalism. A planned economy is not equivalent to socialism, because there is planning under capitalism too; a market economy is not capitalism, because there are markets under socialism too. Planning and market forces are both means of controlling economic activity." Since then, China has embarked more firmly on its journey of market-oriented reform.

The 14th National Congress of the CPC, which was convened in October 1992, decided that building a socialist market economy as the overarching goal of reforms on China's economic system. In November 1993, the 3rd Plenary Session of the 14th CPC Central Committee adopted the *Decision of the CPC Central Committee on Some Issues Concerning the Establishment of a Socialist Market Economy System.* According to this Decision, a socialist market economy system should allow the market to play a fundamental role in the allocation of resources under the macro-regulation of the State. In this new context, China must adhere to the principle of keeping public ownership in a dominant position and having diverse economic sectors develop side by side. The Decision emphasized that the program for building a socialist market economy system included five tasks as follows: (1) to establish a modern enterprise system that respects market rules and features "clearly established ownership, well defined power and responsibility, separation of enterprise from administration, and scientific management"; (2) to build a nationally unified and open market system; (3) to transform the economic functions of the government and establish a sound system for macroeconomic regulation using mainly indirect means; (4) to establish an income distribution system in which distribution according to work is dominant and which gives priority to efficiency with due consideration to fairness; and (5) to establish a multi-level social security system. The Decision, including the above recommendations that still have high relevance in today's China, mapped out the path for China's economic system reform in the mid to late-1990s. After 1994, China implemented a series of reforms on its fiscal and taxation system, its financial, foreign exchange, foreign trade, investment, and circulation systems, achieving significantly positive results. In September 1997, the 15th National Congress of the CPC defined the new system in which public ownership is the mainstay and diverse forms of ownership develop together as the basic economic system in China's primary stage of socialism, which marked a great leap forward in socialist theory and practice.

Since the mid-1980s, China's economy has registered rapid growths, despite interruptions. During the Seventh Five-Year Plan period (1986–1990), the national economy grew at an average annual rate of 7.9%. During the Eighth Five-Year Plan (1991–1995), the national economy grew by an annual average of 11.8%. These years also witnessed the strengthened development of transportation and communications infrastructure, and the rapid development of energy and water infrastructure. The Seventh Five-Year Plan required that within five years, China should: build 3600 km of new railroads, add a track to 3300 km of existing railroads, and electrify 4000 km of railroads; build more than 1600 km of high-speed and first-class (arterial) roads and 10,000 km of second-class roads; dredge and rehabilitate 5000 km of inland waterways; and build 120 deep-water berths and put them into operation. The Eighth Five-Year Plan proposed to build, expand, and rebuild a great many large and medium-sized power stations (including hydro, thermal and nuclear power stations), coal mines, oil fields, railroad and highways, ports, airports, communication trunk lines, water conservancy and other major projects (Office of the Finance and Economy Committee of National People's Congress 2008). In 1988, China's first expressway, the Shanghai-Jiading Expressway, was completed and opened to traffic; and in the same year, the Gezhouba Water Conservancy Project was completed. These achievements show that China's infrastructure development had reached a new level.

In retrospection, during the 15 years from 1978 to 1993, China's economic reform suffered many setbacks but continued to move forward from expanding the autonomy of enterprises to the 1988 Price Reform and to the goal of establishing a socialist market economy. Opinions divided on planning and market economy, but at the decisive moment, the CPC and the central government made a wise and correct choice, firmly taking the course of market-oriented reform.

5.2.3 Infrastructure Development During Market-Oriented Reform in Full Swing (1994–2012)

After the 3rd Plenary Session of the 14th CPC Central Committee, China's market-oriented reform proceeded in full swing, starting with the reform on its fiscal and taxation system. In 1980, China rolled out a new budget management system dividing income and expenditure between the central government and local governments and holding each side responsible for balancing budgets, which was the first version of the "fiscal division system". Since 1982, this system was modified, and according to the revised version, part of local government revenues must be submitted to the central government based on the ratio of local revenues to local expenditures. In

1985, the budget management system was further modified, which divided the central and local government revenues according to tax types, and divided the central and local government expenditures according to their subordination in line with the 1983 policy to substitute tax payment for profit submission (tax for profit). In 1988, as the management contract system was widely implemented by State-owned enterprises, China rolled out as many as six methods of fiscal sharing.

As time went on, the fiscal division system gradually showed its weaknesses. Although through this reform initiative, China had changed the centralized management of fiscal budgets and mobilized local enthusiasm for economic development, the new system required frequent "negotiations" between the central government and local governments and lacked transparency. In addition, the lack of effective supervision by the central government tempted local governments to conceal their fiscal revenues and transfer a large amount of revenues out of the budget system (and hence called extra-budgetary revenues). In the early 1990s, this system created a new problem that aroused great concern among policy makers: the share of central government revenues in GDP and the share of central government revenues in total national revenues continued to drop, while the local extra-budgetary revenues grew rapidly. This has greatly weakened the authority of the central government and its ability to regulate the economy (Zhang 2011).

As a result, China began to implement a new tax-sharing system in 1994, aiming to establish a fiscal budget management system adapted to the development of market economy. Under this new system, a larger proportion of revenues from the main tax (VAT) went to the central government while the basic ratio between central and local government expenditures was kept unchanged. At the same time, the interests of local governments under the original system were protected through tax rebates. The tax-sharing system optimized the fiscal relationship between the central and local governments, significantly increased the share of central government revenues, and eliminated the incentive for local governments to conceal their revenues. The transitional scheme of transfer payment that began in 1995 also laid the foundation for fiscal equalization across regions. More importantly, since VAT is a direct reflection of economic growth, making VAT the main tax is a good incentive for local governments to develop their local economy. Since the mid-1990s, local governments have used income tax exemptions, low land-use prices, and infrastructure improvements to attract investment and promote local economic growth, fueling "competition for growth" (Zhang and Zhou 2008). It proved that the tax-sharing reform has significantly changed the motivation of local governments and injected new impetus into China's economic growth.

On December 11, 2001, China formally became a member of the World Trade Organization (WTO), which began a new chapter of China's open development. Before and after China's accession to the WTO, China systematically revised the laws and regulations related to foreign trade to make them compatible with WTO rules. For example, in 2004, China amended the Foreign Trade Law of the People's Republic of China, liberalizing the right to operate foreign trade. The improvement of the legal system advanced the market economy system (Jiang 2019). Since China's accession to the WTO, China had reduced or eliminated its tariff and non-tariff barriers, and foreign investors' access to the Chinese market has been widened. All these have helped realize the rapid development of foreign trade and accelerated the influx of FDI. In this context, the economy of coastal areas grew rapidly, but the gap between the coastal and hinterland areas widened at the same time.

To bridge the development gap between different regions and achieve the goal of common prosperity as soon as possible, China introduced a series of regional development strategies: the Western Development Strategy in 2000, the strategy of revitalizing old industrial bases in Northeastern China and other parts of the country in 2003, and the decision to boost the rise of central China in 2004. These region-specific strategies boosted infrastructure construction and economic development in Northeastern, Central, and Western China, and helped narrow the development gap between these regions and the rich coastal areas.

After the mid-1990s, China enjoyed rapid economic growth. During the Ninth Five-Year Plan period (1996–2000), its national economy grew at an average annual rate of 8.6%, and during the Tenth Five-Year Plan period (2001–2005), its national economy grew at an average annual rate of 9.8%. Even in 1998 and 1999, amid and right after the Asian financial crisis, China's annual growth rate was close to 8%, much higher than other East Asian countries. During those years, China also made significant achievements in infrastructure development. In terms of transportation infrastructure, the Ninth Five-Year Plan proposed that by 2000, the mileage of China's railroads should reach 68,000 km, of which 34% should be double-track rails and 27% electrified; the mileage of roads should reach 1.23 million kilometers; the throughput of sea ports should come to one billion tons; and the total air transportation turnover should come to 14 billion ton-kilometers. The Tenth Five-Year Plan then proposed that by 2005, the mileage of roads should reach 1.6 million kilometers, including 25,000 km of expressways; the mileage of railroads should reach 75,000 km; and there should be 800 deep-water berths at sea ports. This decade also witnessed the launch and completion of many major projects, including the Beijing-Kowloon Railway opened in 1996, Shanghai Pudong International Airport officially put into operation in 1999, the West–East Power Transmission Project started in 2001, the main component of Xiaolangdi water conservancy project completed in 2001, the first West–East Gas Pipeline put into operation in 2004, and the first phase of Yangshan Deepwater Port of Shanghai International Shipping Center completed in 2005.

The rapid growth of China's economy also caused some environmental problems and social conflicts. The wealth gap, environmental pollution, resource depletion, and developmental imbalances between regions challenged the sustainability of economic development. In the first years of the twenty-first century, China's industrial sulfur dioxide emissions continued to rise and reached a historical high, totaling 22,348,000 tons, in 2006 (refer to the website of NBS). From 2003 to 2009, the Gini coefficient[2] of the distribution of household disposable income per capita stayed

[2] The Gini coefficient, also known as the Gini index or Gini ratio, is an internationally used measure of statistical dispersion intended to represent the income inequality within a nation or a social group. The coefficient can take any values between 0 to 1. The closer it is to 0, the more equal an income distribution is.

above 0.48 in most years and above the "picket line" of 0.40 for a long time (refer to the website of NBS). These problems sounded an alarm for China's economic model and had a direct impact on its subsequent reforms.

In 2003, then Chinese President Hu Jintao proposed the whole nation to implement the Scientific Outlook on Development, a principle that puts people in the first place, calls for comprehensive, balanced, and sustainable development, and promotes across-the-board economic, social, and human development. In 2006, the Eleventh Five-Year Plan was released, which calls for the comprehensive implementation of the Scientific Outlook on Development to accelerate economic transformation, realize harmony between economic development on one hand and population, resources, and the environment on the other. Most notably, the Plan required strict environmental performance assessment and the accountability of government officials for environmental health. This change in the method of official performance evaluation significantly affected local officials' behaviors, and was of great practical importance for reducing pollution emissions and improving environmental quality. In his report to the 17th National Congress of the CPC in 2007, Hu Jintao pointed out that the Scientific Outlook on Development takes development as its essence, putting people first as its core, comprehensive, balanced, and sustainable development as its basic requirement, and overall consideration as its fundamental approach. The Scientific Outlook on Development stands for the direction for further reform and development of China's economy.

In the autumn of 2008, the global financial crisis broke out in the United States and spread rapidly around the world, dumping the global economy into recession. China's economy was severely hit, and its export took a sharp downturn, with many enterprises shutting down and unemployment rising sharply. At this critical moment, the Chinese government promptly implemented a series of fiscal and monetary policies to expand domestic demand and stabilize the economy, injecting a total of 4 trillion RMB yuan into the market liquidity, in which about 1.5 trillion RMB yuan was invested in infrastructure construction (railroads, highways, airports, and water infrastructure) (Zhang 2020). In 2009, China issued a plan for adjusting and revitalizing its key industries, mainly manufacturing industries such as steel, automobiles, equipment, and IT, to mitigate the impact of the recent financial crisis on China's economy.

During the Eleventh Five-Year Plan period (2006–2010), the transformation of China's economy did not hold back its rapid economic growth, with the national economy growing at an average annual rate of 11.3%, and even registering an average annual rate of over 9% during the global financial crisis in 2008–2009. These five years saw not only the fastest economic growth over 70 years since the founding of the People's Republic of China, but also the fastest development of the infrastructure. As it gave priority to the development of the transportation industry, the Eleventh Five-Pear Plan encouraged efforts to build infrastructure such as special passenger rail lines, national expressways, and port transit systems, and promoted the construction of energy infrastructure such as large hydropower stations, power grids, and oil and gas pipelines. In this regard, China achieved remarkable outcomes: the Three Gorges Dam whose main project was completed in 2006 and put into operation in 2012, the Qinghai-Tibet Railway opened to traffic in 2006, the Beijing-Tianjin Intercity Railway opened in 2008, and the Beijing-Shanghai High Speed Railway which was put into operation in 2011 and marked China's entry into an era of high-speed rails.

5.2.4 Infrastructure Development in the New Normal Stage of Economic Development (2013–2019)

After the financial crisis in 2008, global recovery had been very weak. Some developed countries, trapped in deep recession, have tried to bring manufacturing back through trade protection to boost their domestic economy, and many developing countries were mired in the debt crisis. China, too, was confronted with a series of economic problems: weak overseas demand led to a slowdown in export; domestic labor and land costs, and environmental standards were rising; and new economic growth points are missing. Disrupted by the domestic and international troubles, China's economy has since then turned away from track of fast growth and declined steadily.

In 2013, the Central Committee of the CPC decided that China's economy had entered a difficult period when the country had to deal with the slowdown in economic growth, make difficult structural adjustments, and absorb the negative effects of previous economic stimulus policies. In November 2013, the 3rd Plenary Session of the 18th CPC Central Committee was held and adopted the *Decision on Some Major Issues Concerning Comprehensively Deepening the Reform*, which emphasized that economic system reform was the focus of deepening China's reform comprehensively, and that the market must play a decisive role in the allocation of resources and the government must play its own role better. The Decision is an important document that has brought together and mobilized the whole Party and society to deepen China's reform in all aspects. At the 19th National Congress of the CPC held in October 2017, General Secretary Xi Jinping proposed for the first time that as socialism with Chinese characteristics has entered a new era, the principal contradiction facing Chinese society would be that between unbalanced and inadequate development and the people's ever-growing needs for a better life. He made it clear that the overarching goal of deepening reform should be to improve and develop the system of socialism with Chinese characteristics and modernize China's system and capacity for governance. He also stressed the strategic focus, priorities, and direction of the national drive to deepen reform. In short, in the report to the 19th National Congress, Xi Jinping correctly described China's reality and offered the direction for China's future reform in every field.

On this basis, China has taken an important step forward in its development and opening-up. In 2013, China launched its Belt and Road Initiative, which has not only cemented the economic and trade ties with countries and regions along the Belt and Road, but also brought new development opportunities for many Chinese cities and enabled China's infrastructure construction industry to increase its global presence. Since 2014, China has launched a series of national strategies and regional development initiatives for the Beijing-Tianjin-Hebei region (2014), the Yangtze Economic Belt (2016), the Guangdong-Hong Kong-Macao Greater Bay Area (2017), and integration of the Yangtze River Delta (2018). All these efforts aimed to foster new economic growth points while promoting coordinated regional development.

From 2013 to 2019, China's national economy grew at an average annual rate of 7.0%, a solid foundation for realizing the goal of the doubling of GDP and income of urban and rural residents per capita by 2020 based on the 2010 level. During these years, China's infrastructure development also came to a new era. In 2013, Phase I of the Eastern Line of the South-North Water Transfer Project was officially put into use; in the same year, the Ministry of Industry and Information Technology (MIIT) issued 4G licenses; in 2014, Phase I of the Middle Line of the South-North Water Transfer Project was put into use; in 2016, the Five-hundred-meter Aperture Spherical Telescope (FAST), the world's largest single-aperture radio telescope, was completed and became operational, and several national data centers were launched based on it; in 2018, the Hong Kong-Zhuhai-Macao Bridge, the world's longest sea-crossing bridge, was opened to traffic; and in the same year, the third line of the West–East Gas Pipeline project (the eastern and western sections) was completed and put into operation. By the end of 2018, China had 140,000 km of expressways and 29,000 km of high-speed rails, ranking first in the world in both aspects. In 2019, Beijing Daxing International Airport was officially opened, and in the same year, MIIT issued 5G commercial licenses.

In December 2018, the Central Economic Work Conference held in Beijing reiterated that China should "accelerate the launch of commercial 5G operations and strengthen the construction of new infrastructure projects such as artificial intelligence, industrial Internet, and IoT". The 2019 Report on the Work of the Government by the State Council also emphasized the need to "more quickly build next-generation information and communication infrastructure, and spread the use of information network technologies." In early 2020, in the face of the raging COVID-19, the Chinese government explicitly advocated the development of next-generation infrastructure as a policy tool to stabilize economic development, which gave a strong boost to the development of new infrastructure. It is certain that, in the future, China's infrastructure will be upgraded and transformed. Traditional infrastructure that relies on steel and concrete and extensive use of labor will give way to new infrastructure supported by Internet and digital technology which will integrate with the real economy to create new economic growth points. In short, China's infrastructure development has shifted from rapid expansion to high-quality development.

References

Chen, Z.: Records of the Formation of the 24 Ministries of the State Council. CPC History Publishing House, Beijing (2009)

Hu, S.: The Relationship Between the Central Government and Local Governments in Economic Development: A Study on the Changes of China's Fiscal System. Shanghai SDX Joint Publishing Company, Shanghai (2001)

Lin, Y., Cai, F., Li, Z.: The China Miracle: Development Strategy and Economic Reform (Revised). Shanghai SDX Joint Publishing Company, Shanghai (2002)

Murphy, K.M., Shleifer, A., Vishny, R.W.: The transition to a market economy: pitfalls of partial reform. Quart. J. Econ. **107**(1), 889–906 (1992)

Office of the Finance and Economy Committee of the National People's Congress, and Department of Development Planning of the National Development and Reform Commission.: A Compilation of Important Documents on the Five-Year Plan for National Economic and Social Development Since the Founding of the People's Republic of China. Beijing, China Democracy and Legal System Press (2008)

Wu, J.: Economic Reform in Contemporary China. Shanghai Far East Publishing House, Shanghai (2004)

Wu, C., Dong, Z.: The Economic History of the People's Republic of China, 1949–1952. Social Sciences Academic Press, Beijing (2010)

Xi, J.: Speech at the Celebration of the 40th Anniversary of Reform and Opening-up. People's Publishing House, Beijing (2018)

Xi, J.: Speech at the Celebration of the 70th Anniversary of the Founding of the People's Republic of China. Beijing, People's Publishing House (2019)

Xiao, D.: Finding the Path: China's Economic Reform from 1978 to 1992. China Social Sciences Press, Beijing (2019)

Yuan, B.: The memoir of Yuan Baohua. Chapter 7 The Days and Nights of Negotiations in the Soviet Union. China Economic & Trade Herald, vol. 11, pp. 75–77. (2019)

Zhang, J., Zhou, L.: Competing for Growth: The Political Economy of China's Growth. Gezhi Publishing House, Shanghai (2008)

Zhang, J.: "Zhu Rongji and His Revenue-sharing System." Xinmin Weekly, 2011–10–19

Zhang, P.: Detailed Interpretations on the RMB 4 trillion stimulus package: a package should be further adjusted in implementation. 2009–03–06, www.chinanews.com/cj/gncj/news/2009/03-06/1590872.shtml. Accessed 15 Jan 2020

Chapter 6
Infrastructure and Market Integration: From the Perspective of Inter-connectivity by High-Speed Rails

People come and go only for benefits.
—Sima Qian, Records of the Grand Historian

This chapter explores the impact of infrastructure development on labor market integration in China through the inter-connectivity of cities by high-speed rails. This chapter conducts an econometric analysis based on theoretical models that estimate the parameters using the balanced panel data of China's "city pairs" from 2002 to 2015 and the DID method. This study finds that inter-city connectivity by high-speed rails can significantly reduce the wage gap between cities, and the effect is more pronounced between cities that are 100–900 km apart, implying that the expansion of China's high-speed rail network promotes labor market integration between cities. Further research finds that labor market integration can be realized through increasing the flow of labor in the secondary and tertiary industries.

6.1 Motivation

6.1.1 Market Fragmentation Undermining the Economy

China's economy has grown rapidly since the launch of reform and opening-up. From 1978 to 2019, the average annual growth of China's GDP was as high as 9.4%. In 2019, China's GDP reached 99 trillion RMB yuan with its GDP per capita reaching 70,892 RMB yuan, the second highest in the world. At the same time, the socialist market economy with Chinese characteristics has continued to improve. China has

The study of this chapter was first presented at the International Seminar on Joint Research by East China University of Science and Technology and Tokyo Keizai University: Possibilities of Smart Cities hosted by Tokyo Keizai University, Japan in February 2018. The author would like to acknowledge the valuable inputs of Prof. Masahiro Fukushi, Prof. Luo Huanzhen, Prof. Aoki Ryo, Prof. Wu Bojun, and Prof. Wu Yuming.

C. Pan, *Urban Infrastructure and Economic Development in China*, Public Economy and Urban Governance in China, https://doi.org/10.1007/978-981-99-6629-5_6

built a host of markets, including commodity markets, capital markets, and the labor market, which have basically systematized nationwide, laying a solid foundation for China to leverage its economies of scale.

However, it must be noted that market fragmentation still threatens to prevent China from taking advantage of its economies of scale. Young (2000) found that continued reform, and growing interregional competition between duplicative industries, threatened the profitability of these industrial structures, leading local governments to impose a variety of interregional barriers to trade. Thus, the reform process has led to the fragmentation of the domestic market and the distortion of regional production away from patterns of comparative advantage. Poncet (2003) found from China's provincial data (1987–1997) that even if Chinese provinces still rely more on goods from the rest of China than on international imports, provincial borders matter more and more inside the country in the sense that they imply greater discontinuities in the Chinese domestic market. Hsieh et al. (2009) further pointed out that China's market fragmentation will lead to misallocation of resources, thereby lowering the aggregate TFP.

Some statistical analyses suggest that the labor market is more fragmented than commodity and capital markets (Zhao and Xiong 2009). Cai and Yang (2000) pointed out that labor market fragmentation is mainly caused by the institutional barriers left over by the traditional economic system and the pressure of interest groups in cities. Chen and Lu (2008) believed that although the economic policies that lead to labor market fragmentation have helped protect the interests of local people, they widened the rural–urban income gap, thus impeding the urbanization in China. Poncet (2005) also believed that trade protectionist policies that pursue a dual objective of socio-economic stability preservation and fiscal revenues maximization are the key factors behind inter-regional market barriers in China.

6.1.2 Contributions of Railways to Market Integration

Since the Industrial Revolution, the expansion of railways has greatly reduced transportation costs and improved transportation efficiency. Railways were an important driving force for expanding markets and promoting market integration, and played a key role in the surge of capitalist economies.

Slaughter (2001), O'Rourke and Williamson (1999) found that railways reduced regional price gap of goods (such as grains and salt) and facilitated the integration of commodity markets. Andrabi and Kuehlwein (2010) found a sharp price convergence in British Indian grain markets from 1861 to 1920. After analyzing railway construction and grain prices in various parts of India, they believed that railways seemed capable of explaining only about 20% of the decline in price dispersion, which means that India's railway construction drove the integration of regional agricultural commodity markets.

In the second half of the twentieth century, another breakthrough was made in the transportation sector: high-speed rails. In 1964, the world's first high-speed rail network, the Shinkansen in Japan, was opened. This network linking up various parts of Japan is the first commercial operated high-speed rail network in the world. The Shinkansen exerted a huge impact on Japan's economy, significantly improving the transportation of passengers and goods, forming a "4-hour traffic circle" that connects the industrial and commercial belts of Keihin, Chukyo, and Hanshin, as well as cities between them, and driving the formation of Japan's coastal city clusters and market integration among those cities.

Since the 1990s, European countries like France, Germany, the United Kingdom, Italy, and Spain have also engaged in massive construction of high-speed rails, and the European high-speed rail network has grown remarkably, which facilitated the flow of factors of production and people-to-people exchanges between European countries, and laid a material foundation for European economic integration and the formation of the Eurozone.

6.1.3 China's Development of High-Speed Rails

China's high-speed rail system has grown fast, though it came later. In China's own definition, China's high-speed rails are a new type of "passenger railways supporting speeds equal and/or higher than 250 km/h whose initial operating speed is not less than 200 km/h". (Refer to the website of National Railway Administration: http://www.nra.gov.cn/.) In 2004, China issued its "Medium and Long-term Railway Network Development Plan", aiming to build a high-speed rail network consisting of "four vertical lines and four horizontal lines" and running more than 12,000 km, and the target speed is 200 km per hour and more. This Plan is a guideline for the development of China's high-speed rails.

The "four vertical lines" refer to: (1) the Beijing-Shanghai passenger line, connecting Beijing, Tianjin and cities in the eastern coastal region, most importantly the economically advanced Yangtze River Delta; (2) the Beijing-Wuhan-Guangzhou-Shenzhen passenger line, connecting Northern and Southern China; (3) the Beijing-Shenyang-Harbin (Dalian) passenger line, connecting Northeastern China and areas inside the Shanhaiguan Pass; and (4) the Hangzhou-Ningbo-Ningbo-Fuzhou-Shenzhen passenger line, connecting the Yangtze River Delta, the Pearl River Delta, and the southeastern coastal areas.

The "four horizontal lines" refer to: (1) the Xuzhou-Zhengzhou-Lanzhou passenger line, connecting Northwestern and Eastern China; (2) the Hangzhou-Nanchang-Changsha passenger line, connecting Central and Eastern China; (3) the Qingdao-Shijiazhuang-Taiyuan passenger line, connecting Northern and Eastern China; and (4) the Nanjing-Wuhan-Chongqing-Chengdu passenger line, connecting Southwestern and Eastern China.

On August 1, 2008, China's first high-speed rail with independent intellectual property rights and world-class technology, the Beijing-Tianjin Intercity Railway, was opened to traffic, marking the arrival of China's era of high-speed rails. On

December 26, 2009, the Wuhan-Guangzhou section of the Beijing-Guangzhou High-speed Railway was opened to traffic. It is the first high-speed rail in China that supports an average speed of 350 km per hour and the maximum speed of 394 km per hour, which means that the travel from Wuhan to Guangzhou on this passenger line would be reduced from 11 h to around 3 h. It was then the fastest and most densely operating high-speed rail system worldwide. Soon later, the Zhengzhou-Xi'an High-speed Railway (part of the Xuzhou-Zhengzhou-Lanzhou passenger line), the Shanghai-Nanjing High-speed Railway, the Shanghai-Hangzhou High-speed Railway, and the Beijing-Shanghai High-speed Railway were also opened to traffic.

China's high-speed rails, mainly the four vertical and four horizontal lines, have connected its major cosmopolitan cities (including Beijing, Tianjin, Shanghai, Wuhan, Shenzhen, and Changsha), provincial capitals, and other cities into a network, greatly shortening the travel time and distance between all these cities and promoting economic and people-to-people exchanges between regions. By the end of 2019, China's high-speed rail network has covered 30 provinces (including autonomous regions and municipalities), with the total operating mileage reaching 35,000 km, the longest in the world.

In recent years, the economic effects of high-speed rails have become a common interest of scholars. Some believe that high-speed rails reduce transportation costs and improve resource allocation, thereby promoting economic growth, while others believe that high-speed rails would produce a "siphon effect": the reduction of transportation costs will lead to the loss of production factors and further absorption of scarce resources such as human resources by large cities, thus causing economic shocks to small and medium-sized cities along the lines. No doubt, China's initiative to build high-speed rails is an important opportunity and valuable evidence for the study of the economic effects of infrastructure.

6.1.4 Research Questions

As mentioned above, market fragmentation between regions has become a major barrier for China to leverage its advantage in economies of scale. Historical evidence has shown that railway construction, or the expansion of its railway network, is a positive factor in promoting country's market integration. Then, has the expansion of China's high-speed rail network promoted market integration in this country? Considering that China's labor market has a lower degree of integration than the commodity market and capital market, and that China's high-speed rails are mainly passenger lines, another key question is: does the expansion of China's high-speed rail network promote the integration of the labor market? If intercity income gaps are used to reflect the degree of labor market integration (i.e., a wide wage gap indicates a low level of labor market integration), then the question above can be understood as: is the income gap between two cities connected by a high-speed rail is smaller than the gap between two cities not connected by any high-speed rail? If the answer is yes, then the connectivity supported by high-speed rails promotes labor market integration between cities.

Figure 6.1 shows the coefficient of variation (CV, or standard deviation/mean value) of wage levels between China's prefectural cities and the number of cities with high-speed rail stations from 2002 to 2015. The figures shows that as more and more cities have high-speed rail stations, the CV of wages between cities has continued to decline.

Figure 6.2 shows the mean value of the income gap (refer to Sect. 6.2.2 for the method of measurement) between paired prefecture-level cities (refer to Sect. 6.2.2 for the construction of city pairs) and the proportion of city pairs with access to high-speed rails from 2002 to 2015. The figure shows that as more "city pairs" gain access to high-speed rails, the mean value of income gap between paired cities has continued to decline.

At the same time, the city pairs gaining access to high-speed rails from 2002 to 2005 are taken as the experimental group, while other city pairs are taken as the control group. Figure 6.3 shows that, from 2002 to 2015, the mean value of income gap between paired cities in the experimental group is always larger than the control group. Before the massive building of high-speed rails around China in 2008, the mean values of income gaps between city pairs in the experiment group and the control group moved along in parallel. After 2008, especially in the period between 2008 and 2012, the mean values of income gap between paired cities in experimental group declined faster. This highly probably means that the experimental group has a smaller income gap than the control group after the massive expansion of the high-speed rail network, if common changes happening to the experimental group and the control group are excluded from consideration.

The above changes show that, driven by the expansion of the high-speed rail network, labor markets are converging. But is there any causal relationship between

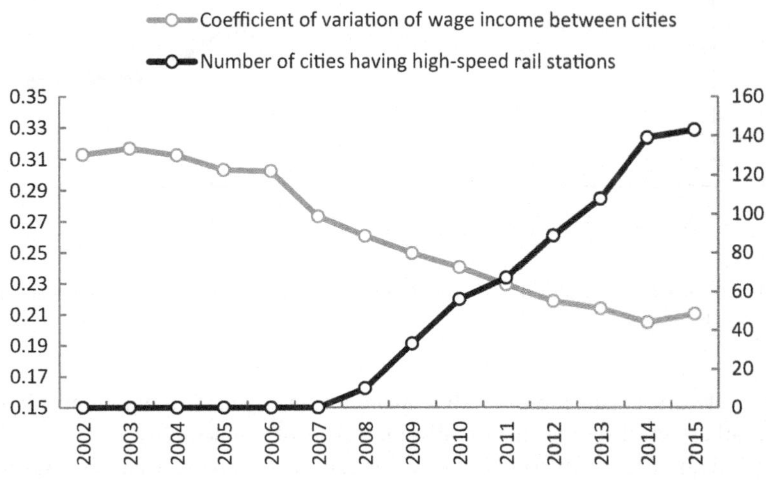

Fig. 6.1 Coefficient of variation of wage income and number of cities with high-speed rail stations

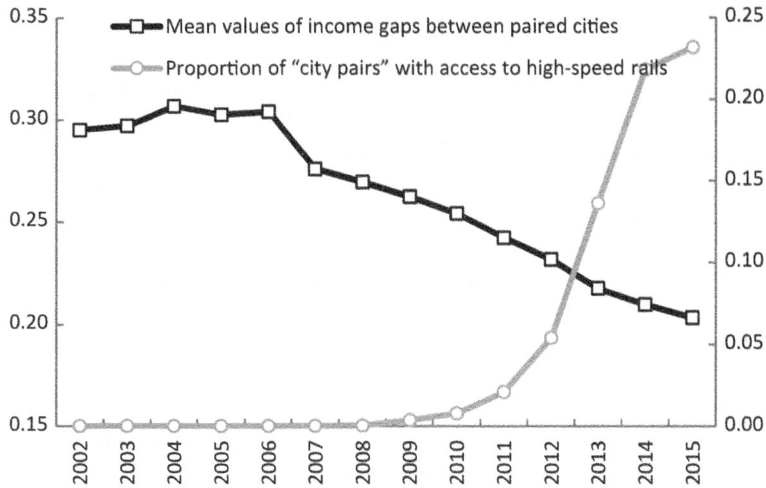

Fig. 6.2 Mean value of income gap between paired cities and the proportion of city pairs with access to high-speed rails

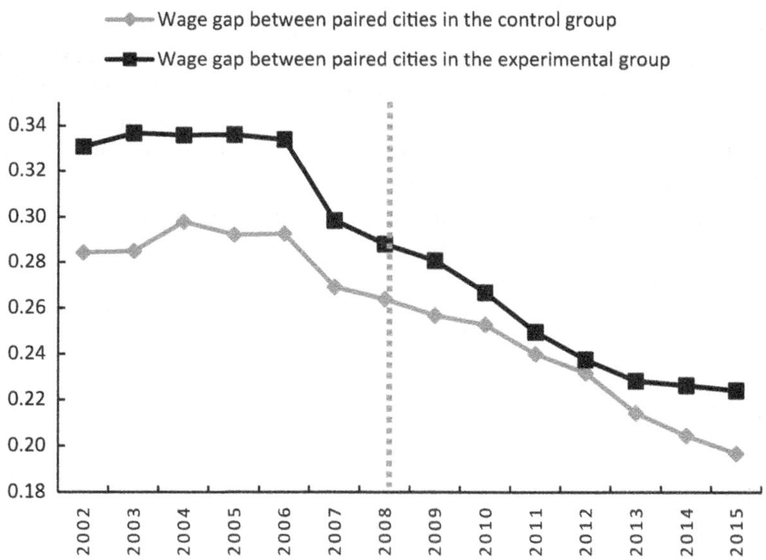

Fig. 6.3 Changes to the mean value of income gap between paired cities in the control group and the experimental group

railway network expansion and labor market convergence? Is the convergence of labor markets in different cities really the result of connectivity through building high-speed rails? If the answer is yes, how much can the connectivity explain? Obviously, these questions need to be answered through empirical research. Therefore, the following section is dedicated to exploring the effects of HSR connectivity by building a DID econometric model.

6.2 Empirical Research Methodology

6.2.1 Theoretical Analysis and Model Setting

In order to set the econometric model reasonably, a theoretical model is first established that reflects the relationship between inter-city income gaps and transportation costs. Suppose an individual who is born in city i but works in city j $(j \neq i)$ has a utility function:

$$u_{ij} = w_j^{\alpha} \cdot X_j^{\beta} \cdot C_{ij}^{\gamma} \cdot \varepsilon_{ij} \tag{6.1}$$

In which i is the city of birth; j is the city of work; w is the wage level; X is the urban factor that affects the utility; C is the transportation cost from the city of birth to the city of work; ε is the error term; constants $\alpha > 0$, $\beta > 0$, $\gamma < 0$ represent the elasticity of variables affecting personal utility. Accordingly, the utility function of the individual who was born in city i and works in city i can be obtained:

$$u_{ii} = w_i^{\alpha} \cdot X_i^{\beta} \cdot \varepsilon_{ii} \tag{6.2}$$

Variable C is not included on the right side of Eq. (6.2) as individuals working in the city of birth do not have to bear any transportation cost. Suppose, in equilibrium, no one can achieve utility improvement by traveling between cities, or in other words, any individual born in city i, whether he is working in city i or city j $(j \neq i)$, will get the same utility. So, divide Eq. (6.1) by Eq. (6.2) to get the equilibrium condition:

$$\frac{u_{ij}}{u_{ii}} = \left(\frac{w_j}{w_i}\right)^{\alpha} \cdot \left(\frac{X_j}{X_i}\right)^{\beta} \cdot C_{ij}^{\gamma} \cdot \left(\frac{\varepsilon_{ij}}{\varepsilon_{ii}}\right) = 1 \tag{6.3}$$

Take the logarithm of both sides, and then:

$$ln\left(\frac{w_j}{w_i}\right) = -\frac{\beta}{\alpha}\ln\left(\frac{X_j}{X_i}\right) - \frac{\gamma}{\alpha}\ln C_{ij} - \frac{1}{\alpha}\ln\left(\frac{\varepsilon_{ij}}{\varepsilon_{ii}}\right) \tag{6.4}$$

Equation (6.4) shows that $-\gamma/\alpha > 0$, so when the transportation cost C decreases, the income gap between two cities will decrease accordingly. The above theoretical inferences lay the foundation for an econometric model. Further assume that the transportation cost between two cities decreases after the opening of high-speed rail:

$$lnC_{ijt} = \delta HSR_{ijt} + \eta_{ij} + \lambda_t + \varphi_{ijt} \tag{6.5}$$

In which HSR_{ijt} (high-speed rail) is a dummy variable, indicating whether a high-speed rail is opened between city i and city j ($j \neq i$). "Opened" is while "Not Opened" is 0; coefficient $\delta < 0$; η_{ij} is the fixed effects of the paired city i and city j; λ_t is the fixed effect of year; φ_{ijt} is the random disturbance term. Substitute this function into the equilibrium condition to obtain:

$$ln\left(\frac{w_{jt}}{w_{it}}\right) = \Pi_0 + \Pi_1 \cdot HSR_{ijt} + \Pi_2 \cdot ln\left(\frac{X_{jt}}{X_{it}}\right) + \eta_{ij} + \lambda_t + v_{ijt} \quad (6.6)$$

In which Π_0, Π_1 and Π_2 are all constants. Equation (6.6) constitutes an econometric model that can estimate the impact of HSR connectivity on the income gap between paired cities. The dummy variable HSR_{ijt} reflects the accessibility of each city pair to high-speed rails at different times, so the above model has the characteristics of DID econometric analysis. The coefficient Π_1 represents the impact of the access to high-speed rails on the income gap between the two cities. If the coefficient is in the minus, it means that accessibility to high-speed rails narrows the income gap, thereby promoting the convergence of labor markets of two cities.

6.2.2 *Variable Construction and Data Sources*

(1) Construction of "city pairs"

"City pair" is a main variable of this research. First, a balanced panel data set is constructed based on the 278 cities at the prefecture level and above in China from 2002 to 2015. The 278 cities are paired without repetition to form 38,503 "city pairs", thus forming a set of 38,503 "city pairs". This construction method is consistent with the method of Andrabi and Kuehlwein (2010) who discussed how the construction of railways affects price convergence between districts in British India.

(2) Explained variable: Income gap between paired cities

Income gap between paired cities is the explained variable of this research. Based on the derivation results of the econometric model, logarithm is taken of the ratio of city j with higher income level to city i with lower income level which form a "city pair".

(3) Explanatory variable: Connectivity between paired cities by high-speed rails

Connectivity between paired cities by high-speed rails is the core explanatory variable of this research. The time of each city's accessibility to high-speed rails and the starting time of operation of each high-speed rail line are obtained from the entry "China's high-speed rail" in the real-time updated Baidu Encyclopedia. The dummy variable HSR_{ijt} is set like this: If in year t a high-speed rail is opened to connect city i and city j, then $HSR_{ijt} = 1$, or otherwise $HSR_{ijt} = 0$.

(4) Control variables

To minimize estimation bias due to omission of variables, five control variables are used which are measured by the logarithm of variables relating to paired cities. The numerators are the variables of the higher-income city *j*.

First, the economic development gap between paired cities. A city's GDP per capita is used to measure the level of economic development, and then logarithm is taken of the ratio of GDP per capita between two paired cities to measure the economic development gap between them.

Second, the industrial development gap between paired cities. The ratio of the output of the city's secondary industry to its GDP is used to measure the industrialization level of the city, and then logarithm is taken of the ratio of industrialization level between two paired cities to measure the industrial development gap between them.

Third, the Government size gap between paired cities. The ratio of a city's fiscal expenditures to its GDP used to measure a city's Government size (i.e., the scale of government spending), and then logarithm is taken of the ratio of Government size between two paired cities to measure the Government size gap between them.

Fourth, the investment openness gap between two paired cities. The ratio of the total amount of FDI actually used by the city to its GDP is used to measure the level of investment openness of the city, and then logarithm is taken of the ratio of the openness level between two paired cities to measure the openness gap between them.

Fifth, the education gap between two paired cities. The teacher-student ratio of high schools (including junior and senior high schools) of a city is used to measure the quality of basic education, and then logarithm is taken of the ratio of basic education quality between two paired cities to measure the education gap between them.

(5) Data sources

There are mainly two data sources. The first is China City Statistical Yearbooks, from which relevant data of cities at the prefecture level and above are obtained. The second source is Baidu. The precise opening dates of railways are not officially published. Therefore, the dates when each city gains access to high-speed rails and the year when each city pair is connected by high-speed rails by searching the entry "China's high-speed rails" in Baidu Encyclopedia.

The basic statistics of the above variables are shown in Table. 6.1.

6.3 Analysis of Estimation Results

6.3.1 Estimation of the Impact of HSR Connectivity on the Wage Gap Between Paired Cities

Table 6.2 shows the estimation results of full-sample regression models. Among them, Model (1) does not use control variables and the fixed effect of year, while Model (2) adds the fixed effect of year and Model (3) further adds the control variables

Table 6.1 Basic statistics

Variable	Observation	Average	Standard deviation	Minimum	Maximum
Wage gap between paired cities (logarithm)	532,992	0.2624	0.2159	0.0000	1.7196
Economic development gap between paired cities (logarithm)	530,514	0.4727	0.7224	− 3.1967	3.6282
Industrial development gap between paired cities (logarithm)	531,887	0.0734	0.3348	− 2.1459	2.2853
Government size gap between paired cities (logarithm)	532,164	− 0.1055	0.5911	− 3.4916	3.9193
Openness gap between paired cities (logarithm)	490,853	0.4396	1.7504	− 7.6201	8.8807
Education gap between paired cities (logarithm)	532,162	0.0425	0.2776	− 3.0877	2.9700

to measure the gap between two paired cities. As the F distribution shows, all the models are highly significant. Two conclusions can be drawn from Table 6.2.

First, the coefficient of the variable of HSR connectivity between paired cities is negative and shows a significance level of 1% in each model, which means that compared with city pairs that are not connected by high-speed rails, the wage gap between connected cities is smaller. If this significant correlation is interpreted as a causal effect, it means that the opening of a high-speed rail between the two cities has indeed narrowed the wage gap between them, thereby facilitating labor market convergence. According to the estimation results of Model (1), if a high-speed rail is opened between two cities, then the wage gap between them would shrink by 7.48%. But after adding the fixed effect of year, the coefficient drops from 7.48% to 0.99%, suggesting that, when the fixed effect of year are ignored, the role of HSR connectivity in narrowing the wage gap is overestimate. After adding the control variables, the coefficient drops from 0.99% to 0.68%, which shows that the effect of HSR connectivity on narrowing the income gap between two paired cities is still overestimated when various gaps between cities are ignored.

Second, in Model (3), except for the education gap between paired cities, other control variables are significantly positive, which means that the gaps in economic development, industrial development, government size, and investment openness all affect the wage gap between paired cities. Among them, for every 1% increase in the economic development gap, the wage gap will increase by 6.55%; for every 1% increase in the industrial development gap, the wage gap will increase by 1.83%; for

Table 6.2 Estimation results of the impact of HSR connectivity on the wage gap between paired cities

	Model (1)	Model (2)	Model (3)
Explained variable	Income gap between two paired cities (logarithm)		
HSR connectivity of a city pair	– 0.0748*** [0.0013]	– 0.0099*** [0.0014]	– 0.0068*** [0.0013]
Economic development gap between paired cities (logarithm)			0. 0655*** [0.0010]
Industrial development gap between paired cities (logarithm)			0.0183*** [0.0015]
Government size gap between paired cities (logarithm)			0.0356*** [0.0007]
Openness gap between paired cities (logarithm)			0.0044*** [0.0002]
Education gap between paired cities (logarithm)			[0.0016] 0.0011
Fixed effects of year	No	Yes	Yes
Fixed effects of city pair	Yes	Yes	Yes
Observation	532,992	532,992	488,722
Within-group R2	0.0170	0.1072	0.1634
F distribution	3305.1464	1034.3189	958.7330
p-value	0.0000	0.0000	0.0000

Notes
1. ***, **, * indicate the significance levels of 1%, 5%, and 10% respectively.
2. Values in [ ] are robust standard errors.

every 1% increase in the government size gap, the wage gap will increase by 3.56%; and for every 1% increase in the openness gap, the wage gap will increase by 0.44%. Meanwhile, the education gap has no remarkable effect on the wage gap between two paired cities.

6.3.2 Geographical Distance and HSR Connectivity

The above analysis shows that HSR connectivity can narrow the wage gap between cities, but whether this effect is affected by the geographic distance between cities remains a question. Therefore, city pairs are classified into 5 types based on distance: adjacent cities, cities in the same province, cities within 100 km apart from each other, cities within 100 to 900 km apart from each other, and cities more than 900 km apart from each other. Then, sub-sample regression is made on these five types of city pairs. Table 6.3 shows the effects of HSR connectivity on city pairs with different distances. The estimation results of each control variable are basically consistent with the estimation results of the benchmark Model (3), which indicates that this model has a stable structure.

More importantly, the role of HSR connectivity in narrowing the wage gap is only significant for paired cities that are 100–900 km apart. According to the estimation results of Model (7), HSR connectivity can reduce the wage gap between paired cities by 1.33%. For adjacent cities that are less than 100 km apart or greater than 900 km apart, the coefficient of the variable of HSR connectivity is still negative, but not significant. This may be because high-speed rails are not the best means of travel between cities that are close or far apart. For travel between close cities, people tend to drive cars or take intercity buses or ordinary trains. To travel to farther cities, people may take planes to save time. Therefore, the effect of HSR connectivity mainly exists in city pairs that are separated by medium distances. In conclusion, the estimation results of sub-sample regression by distance further deepen the understanding of the effects of HSR connectivity.

In Table. 6.3, in addition to using full sample, two interaction terms, "HSR connectivity of a city pair × distance of a city pair" and "HSR connectivity of a city pair × squared distance of a city pair", are used to reflect the nonlinear influence of distance changes on the effects of HSR connectivity. Their estimation results are shown in Model (9). The interaction term "HSR connectivity of a city pair × distance of a city pair" is significantly negative, while interaction term "HSR connectivity of a city pair × squared distance of a city pair" is significantly positive, which indicates that as the distance between paired cities increases, the negative effect of HSR connectivity on the wage gap between cities firstly goes up and then gradually weakens. Based on the estimation results of Model (9), a U-shaped curve is drawn to reflect how the HSR connectivity effect changes with the distance between cities (see Fig. 6.4). It can be found that the nonlinear characteristics of this HSR connectivity effect and the estimation results of Models (6) to (8) are consistent.

6.4 Key Findings and Policy Implications

This chapter investigates the impact of HSR connectivity on inter-city labor market integration. Reviewing the historical experience of railway development in other countries and the economic effects of high-speed rails in China, this chapter builds a theoretical model to estimate the relationship between inter-city wage gap and transportation costs. Based on this, an econometric model is set up like the DID method and then the balanced panel data of 38,503 city pairs based on 278 cities at the prefecture level and above collected from 2002 to 2015 are estimated. The research of this chapter has three key findings as follows.

First, overall, HSR connectivity has significantly narrowed the inter-city income gap, thereby promoting inter-city labor market integration. Second, the effect of HSR connectivity firstly goes up and then gradually weakens along with the increase of the distance between cities. This effect is most obvious when the distance between

Table 6.3 Impact of distance between paired cities on HSR connectivity

	Model (4)	Model (5)	Model (6)	Model (7)	Model (8)	Model (9)
Distance between paired cities	Adjacent	Same province	< 100 km	100–900 km	> 900 km	Full sample
Explained variable	Wage gap between paired cities (logarithm)					
HSR connectivity of a city pair	– 0.0087 [0.0055]	0.0023 [0.0051]	– 0.0009 [0.0102]	– 0.0133 [0.0019]	– 0.0023 [0.0019]	– 0.0016 [0.0038]
HSR connectivity of a city pair × distance of a city pair						– 0.0201 [0.0070]
HSR connectivity of a city pair × squared distance of a city pair						0.0115 [0.0028]
Economic development gap between paired cities (logarithm)	0.0671 [0.0048]	0.0456 [0.0044]	0.0415 [0.0113]	0.0643 [0.0017]	0.0662 [0.0013]	0.0655 [0.0010]
Industrial development gap between paired cities (logarithm)	0.0243 [0.0081]	0.0380 [0.0087]	0.0578 [0.0297]	0.0344 [0.0027]	0.012 1 [0.0019]	0.0182 [0.0015]
Government size gap between paired cities (logarithm)	0.0415 [0.0035]	0.0335 [0.0032]	0.0397 [0.0085]	0.0449 [0.0011]	0.0308 [0.0009]	0.0355 [0.0007]
Openness gap between paired cities (logarithm)	0.0020 [0.0010]	- 0.0006 [0.0009]	0.0039 [0.0025]	0.0039 [0.0004]	0.0043 [0.0002]	0.0044 [0.0002]
Education gap between paired cities (logarithm)	– 0.0007 [0.0052]	0.0211 [0.0050]	– 0.005 [0.0125]	– 0.0004 [0.0018]	0.0029 [0.0015]	0.0016 [0.0011]
	Model (4)	Model (5)	Model (6)	Model (7)	Model (8)	Model (9)

(continued)

Table 6.3 (continued)

	Model (4)	Model (5)	Model (6)	Model (7)	Model (8)	Model (9)
Fixed effects of year	Yes	Yes	Yes	Yes	Yes	Yes
Fixed effects of city pair	Yes	Yes	Yes	Yes	Yes	Yes
Observation	18,873	21,786	3421	187,091	298,210	488,722
Within-group R2	0.1572	0.1727	0.1672	0.1642	0.1664	0.1635
F distribution	44.0941	53.3938	8.6254	408.5292	590.1120	872.2990
p-value	0.0000	0.0000	0.0000	0.0000	0.0000	0.0000

Notes

1. ***, **, * correspond to 1%, 5%, and 10% respectively.
2. Values in [ ] are robust standard errors.
3. The geographic distance within the city pair is calculated by GIS and the geodist command of Stata.

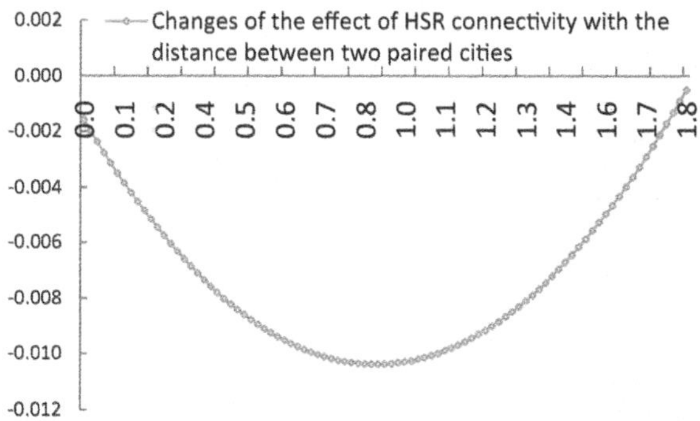

Fig. 6.4 Changes of the HSR connectivity effect with the distance of a city pair

two paired cities is 100–900 km. Third, HSR connectivity has significantly narrowed the inter-city differences of labor in secondary and tertiary industries, which means that HSR connectivity narrows the wage gap by promoting the mobility of labor in secondary and tertiary industries between cities. At the same time, inter-city gaps in economic development, industrial development, government size, openness, and education also significantly affect the wage gap, thereby impacting labor market integration of between cities.

This research has significant theoretical and policy implications. Theoretically, it reveals how and why transportation infrastructure affects market integration, and supports researches on the economic effects of infrastructure in developing countries. In terms of policy significance, this research offers the direction to design and adjust policies to improve market integration, especially government policies for labor market integration. There are three specific recommendations:

First, more high-speed railways should be built so that more people can enjoy the convenience they offer. China should work to transform into a country with a robust transportation network partly by building a high-speed rail network covering large and medium-sized cities across the country. In this way, more regions and more cities can benefit from the free flow and efficient agglomeration of factors, and accelerated market integration will lay a solid foundation for China to leverage its economies of scale.

Second, barriers to labor mobility should be broken down in order to allow high-speed railways to promote market integration. In fact, due to the institutional barriers such as household registration in big cities, the effect of HSR connectivity is rather limited. Therefore, China must take bold reform measures to remove the institutional barriers that hinder the flow of labor and other factors, especially measures to lower the threshold for settlement in big cities and cosmopolitan cities, in order to utilize the positive effects of high-speed railways on market integration.

Third, the current governing approach should be adjusted to cultivate new economic growth points based on local comparative advantages. With the popularization of access to high-speed railways and the removal of institutional barriers, the inter-regional flow of factors such as labor will inevitably increase. Of course, some regions will face the challenges of massive labor outflows and a rapid decline in labor-intensive industries, while others will face massive labor influxes and surging urban commuting demand and housing prices. It is recommended that, in areas which labor flows into, the local governments should actively promote manufacturing and service industries to create more jobs and improve the rendering of public services such as government-subsidized housing. In areas from which labor flows out, the local governments should fully exploit the potential of agriculture, tourism, and resource-based industries, and must not blindly copy the development model of areas with massive labor influxes. In a word, the best solution is to change the traditional development mode, avoid focusing on GDP growth rate only, turn to utilize the comparative advantages, and cultivate new growth points suitable for each region.

References

Andrabi, T., Kuehlwein, M.: Railway and price convergence in British India. J. Econ. History **70**(2), 351–377 (2010)

Cai, F., Yang, T.: The political economy of urban-rural income gap in China. Soc. Sci. China **4** (2000)

Chen, Z., Lu, M.: From segmentation to integration: the political economy of urban–rural economic growth and social harmony. J. Econ. Res. **1** (2008)

Hsieh, C.T., Klenow, P.J.: Misallocation and manufacturing TFP in China and India. Q. J. Econ. **124**(4), 1403–1448 (2009)

O'Rourke, K., Williamson, J.: Globalization and history: the evolution of a nineteenth-century Atlantic economy. MIT Press, Cambridge, MA (1999)

Poncet, S.: Measuring Chinese domestic and international integration. China Econ. Rev. **14**(1), 1–21 (2003)

Poncet, S.: A fragmented China: Measure and determinants of Chinese domestic market disintegration. Rev. Int. Econ. **13**(3), 409–430 (2005)
Slaughter, M.: Does trade liberalization converge factor prices? Evidence from the antebellum transportation revolution. J. Int. Trade. Econ. Dev. **10**(3), 339–362 (2001)
Young, A.: The razor's edge: Distortions and incremental reform in the People's Republic of China. Q. J. Econ. **115**(4), 1091–1135 (2000)
Zhao, Q., Xiong, X.: A comparative analysis of the segmentation of three markets in China: from the perspectives of time and region. J. World Econ. **6** (2009)

Chapter 7
Infrastructure Development on Open Development: From the Perspective of Foreign Direct Investment

China's door will never be closed; it will only open wider.
—Xi Jinping, "Openness for Greater Prosperity, Innovation for a Better Future"

This chapter explores the impact of infrastructure on China's open development from the perspective of FDI. Based on the panel data of China's provincial capitals and prefecture-level cities, this chapter investigates the role of social infrastructure and economic infrastructure in mobilizing FDI inflows. The study finds that foreign capital pays more attention to the level of social infrastructure in a region, while the improvement of economic infrastructure still has a positive effect on FDI. This chapter not only reveals the factors behind the regional distribution of FDI in the context of weak global economic recovery and China's economic structural transformation, but also informs adjustments to infrastructure-related public policies towards a favorable environment for FDI.

7.1 Motivation

7.1.1 Economic Transformation and the Exit of Foreign Capital

FDI is an important foundation of economic globalization and plays a positive role in promoting capital accumulation, technological progress, and economic growth in developing countries. Since its reform and opening-up, and especially since its accession to the WTO in 2001, China has integrated into the global industrial system very fast and become an attractive destination for foreign capital. Since 2010, China has recorded annual FDI inflows exceeding 100 billion US dollars, staying ahead of most other countries in the world.[1] Empirical studies have shown that FDI has

[1] According to World Investment Reports released by UNCTAD, China ranked second, second, first, fourth, and third in terms of FDI flows in 2012, 2013, 2014, 2015, and 2016.

C. Pan, *Urban Infrastructure and Economic Development in China*, Public Economy and Urban Governance in China, https://doi.org/10.1007/978-981-99-6629-5_7

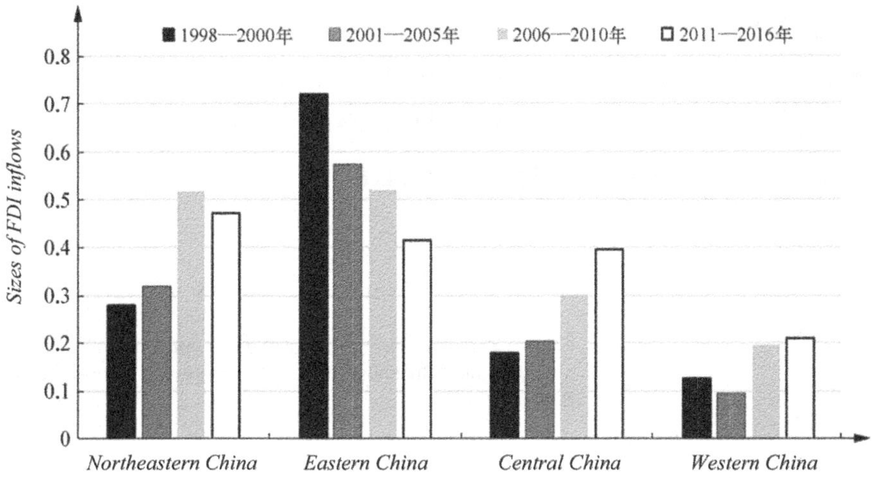

Fig. 7.1 Sizes of FDI inflows in different regions of China in different periods. *Source China Statistical Yearbooks*

promoted China's industrial development and economic growth, and improved the innovation capacity and productivity of local businesses.

However, there are many worrisome news about foreign capital leaving China in recent years. For example, in 2015, Microsoft closed Nokia's factories in Dongguan and Beijing, and laid off about 9000 employees; in 2016, Marks & Spencer withdrew from mainland China; in 2017, hard disk manufacturer Seagate shut down its plant in Suzhou; in January 2018, Nitto Denko (Suzhou) announced to discontinue operation; in April 2018, Samsung closed its Shenzhen factory; and in 2019, Carrefour China sold an 80% equity interest to Suning Tesco.

Figure 7.1 shows the sizes of FDI in different regions of China in different periods. Using the ratios of FDI actually used in Northeastern China, Eastern China, Central China, and Western China[2] to the GDP of the respective region, this research finds that FDI in Eastern China, which leads the country in economic development and has obvious geographical advantages, declined fast. It rose in three other regions in the first three periods, but from 2011 to 2016, it leveled off in Western China and dropped in Northeastern China.

The reasons for some foreign investors to leave China are manifold. First, due to the economic transformation in China and sluggish foreign demand, the stimulus for investment in China's traditional industries has weakened and there is a serious excess of backward production capacity, which deters FDI investment in

[2] For the purpose of this table, Northeastern China includes Heilongjiang, Liaoning, and Jilin; Eastern China includes Beijing, Tianjin, Hebei, Shanghai, Jiangsu, Zhejiang, Fujian, Shandong, Guangdong, and Hainan; Central China includes Shanxi, Anhui, Jiangxi, Henan, Hubei, and Hunan; and Western China includes Inner Mongolia, Guangxi, Chongqing, Sichuan, Guizhou, Yunnan, Tibet, Shaanxi, Gansu, Qinghai, Ningxia, and Xinjiang. See the website of the National Bureau of Bureau of Statistics for more details.

these industries. Second, the prices of factors of production such as labor and land use right have risen rapidly, and FDI in labor-intensive industries has moved away to countries and regions with lower costs, such as Southeast Asia, Central Asia, and Africa. Third, environmental protection has toughened, which forces FDI projects with high energy consumption and high emissions to withdraw from China as they've lost their competitiveness. Fourth, weak domestic innovation capacity deters the inflow of technology-intensive FDI. All in all, these problems indicate that China's development is imbalanced and inadequate.

Therefore, given the sluggish global economic recovery and China's slowdown, it is urgent to implement stronger incentives to attract foreign capital and provide a favorable business environment to promote the continuous inflow of FDI into China.

7.1.2 Research Questions

Economic decentralization and vertical governance have been the core features of China's political and economic governance system for a long time. Under this system, to get promoted, local officials are motivated to improve infrastructure such as transportation, energy, and communications to boost FDI inflows and local economic growth. Local governments are competing to attract investments by improving infrastructure at all costs, and are firmly committed to creating a favorable environment to attract the factors of production (Zhang et al. 2007). However, some recent studies have found that China's infrastructure construction (especially in Western China) is possibly overinvested (Shi and Huang 2014). At the same time, dependence of infrastructure development on debt financing increases financial risks and economic weaknesses (Ansar et al. 2016). Therefore, whether investment in traditional economic infrastructure can still attract FDI inflows under diminishing marginal productivity is the first question this research aims to answer.

At the same time, since basic education, healthcare, culture, and sports cannot directly promote local economic growth in the short term, under the current political and economic system, local governments tend to ignore or neglect the provision of social infrastructure (or public goods and services) such as science, education, culture, and healthcare. The imbalance between economic infrastructure and social infrastructure obviously deters the improvement of human capital in any region (Fu and Zhang 2007). It is highly possible that, given a sound system of economic infrastructure, better social infrastructure can help governments attract FDI inflows and thus raise the level of human capital in a region. Obviously, better human capital means a strong capacity to learn and master imported advanced technologies, which supports initiatives to attract technology-intensive, high value-added FDI (De Gregorio and Lee 1998). Better human capital can not only raise the productivity of multinational corporations, but also reduce the cost of personnel training and turnover, thereby improving the return on capital of multinational corporations. Of course, better social infrastructure will increase labor costs, which has a certain inhibitory effect on FDI in traditional manufacturing. Here comes the second question: Does investment in social infrastructure really help attract FDI inflows? Or, to put it in another way, does FDI flow into areas with better social infrastructure?

This study examines the roles of social infrastructure and economic infrastructure in attracting FDI inflows. The quality of social infrastructure is measured by education and human capital, and the quality of economic infrastructure is measured by transportation infrastructure. On this basis, econometric analysis is carried out using the panel data of Chinese provincial capitals and prefecture-level cities. The estimation results consistently show that the improvement of social infrastructure increases FDI inflows, while economic infrastructure is still a positive factor in attracting FDI.

In short, this research will not only give insights into the dynamics behind the regional distribution of FDI in the context of sluggish global recovery and China's economic transformation, but also aims to inform public policies related to infrastructure development for attracting FDI and promoting all-round open development. At the same time, this research also supports research on the economic effects of infrastructure in developing countries.

7.2 Empirical Research Methodology

7.2.1 Theoretical Analysis and Model Setting

First, a theoretical model is constructed to analyze the impact of social infrastructure and economic infrastructure on return on capital and then their impact on FDI inflow. Assume that regional production function coincides with the Cobb–Douglas production function, and then:

$$Y = AK^{\alpha}(EL)^{\beta}(S)^{1-\alpha-\beta} \tag{7.1}$$

In which Y is the output level; A is the technology level; K is the material capital stock; L is the quantity of labor; E is the social infrastructure, which reflects the level of education and human capital in a region and promotes the increase of output by affecting labor (so EL measures the quantity of effective labor); S is the economic infrastructure which directly affects the output level; α, β and $1 - \alpha - \beta$ stand for the output elasticity (from 0 to 1) of capital, effective labor and infrastructure. Take the partial derivative with respect to K, and the marginal rate of return on capital is:

$$r = \alpha AK^{\alpha-1}(EL)^{\beta}S^{1-\alpha-\beta} \tag{7.2}$$

From Eq. (7.2), it can be derived:

$$\begin{cases} \partial r/\partial E > 0 \\ \partial r/\partial S > 0 \end{cases} \tag{7.3}$$

That means that improvements in both social and economic infrastructure can increase the marginal rate of return on capital, thereby attracting FDI inflows. Then render r into the per-capita form:

$$r = (\alpha A E^{\beta} s^{1-\alpha-\beta})/k^{1-\alpha} \tag{7.4}$$

In which s is the economic infrastructure stock per capita, and k is the physical capital stock per capita. From Eq. (7.4), it can be found that while a smaller k in low-income regions (or poor countries) can increase the marginal rate of return on capital, a better E and a larger s in high-income regions (or rich countries) suppress the relative disadvantage caused by the abundance of capital, which is the key point of the Lucas paradox (Lucas 1990).

According to the above theoretical analysis, using the actual data of China, the equation is obtained as follows:

$$lnFDI_{it} = \gamma_0 + \gamma_1 E_{it} + \gamma_2 S_{it} + \gamma_3 M_{it} + \eta_i + \varepsilon_{it} \tag{7.5}$$

In which $lnFDI_{it}$ is the amount of actually used FDI (i is the province or prefecture-level city, and t is the year); E is the level of social infrastructure; S is the level of economic infrastructure; M is the control variable (see Sect. 7.3.2 for its construction); γ_0, γ_1, γ_2, and γ_3 are all constants; η_i is the fixed effects of provinces or prefecture-level cities (including factors that do not change over time, such as language, culture, and geographic location); and ε_{it} is a random error term. Using the log-linear model, while other conditions remain unchanged, FDIit increases by $\gamma_1\%$ for every 0.01 unit increase in E, while *FDIit* increases by $\gamma_2\%$ for every 0.01 unit increase in S.

7.2.2 Variable Construction and Data Sources

(1) Explained variable: FDI

FDI is the explained variable of this research. First, exchange rates of RMB yuan against the US dollar over the years are used to convert the FDI actually used in each region into RMB amounts, and then the consumer price indexes (CPIs) of each province and prefecture-level city over the years (with 2000 as the base year) are used to deflate the above data (and then logarithms are taken).

(2) Core explanatory variable 1: Level of social infrastructure

The level of social infrastructure is a core explanatory variable of this research. According to existing research, there is currently no recognized method or indicator for measuring the level of regional social infrastructure. For the purpose of this research, the level of social infrastructure in each province and prefecture-level city is measured by education and human capital. The following three variables are estimated.

First, average years of schooling. The index of each province is the weighted average of populations with various education attainments, and the equation is: Average years of schooling = (6 × population aged six and above attending or having attended primary school + 9 × population aged six and above attending or having attended junior high school + 12 × population aged 6 and above attending or having attended senior high school including vocational schools + 16 × population aged 6 and above attending or having attended two-year college and university) ÷ total population aged 6 and above. The statistics of prefecture-level cities are directly from the 2000 Population Census by County and the 2010 China Population Census by County. The average years of schooling is a good measure of a province or city's current level of human capital.

Second, density of university or college students (per 100 students). The ratio of the number of students attending universities or two-year colleges in a province (or prefecture-level city) to the total population at the end of year of the province (or prefecture-level city). University/college students constitute a key indicator of high-quality human capital, so this variable reflects accurately the level of high-quality human capital in a province or city.

Third, ratio of teachers to students at all levels (per 10,000 students). A factor analysis is made on the ratio of teachers to students in primary schools, junior high schools, senior high schools and universities/colleges in each province and prefecture-level city. Thus, the first principal component of provincial and prefecture-level city data is obtained: the teacher-student ratio. Teachers are the most important educational resources, and current educational resources are the input factors for creating future human capital (Wu and Zhang 2017), so this ratio is used as the proxy for future human capital.

(3) Core explanatory variable 2: Level of economic infrastructure

The level of economic infrastructure is another core explanatory variable of this research, and is measured by transportation infrastructure. Both roads and railways are important components of transportation infrastructure, and there is a high positive correlation between them. Therefore, a factor analysis is made on the road mileage per capita (of which the logarithm is then taken) and railway mileage per capita (of which the logarithm is then taken) in each province. Then, the first principal component, provincial transportation infrastructure index, is estimated and used as the proxy for measuring the regional level of transportation infrastructure.

Given that there is no systematic road and railway mileage data for prefecture-level cities, the total highway and railway mileages of each province are broken down among the prefecture-level cities according to their relative economic scale (by GDP) in order to estimate the road and railway mileages of the prefecture-level cities. Based on these estimates, a factor analysis and the first principal component analysis are made to obtain the transportation infrastructure index of each prefecture-level city.

(4) Control variables

To minimize the bias caused by omission of relevant variables, two control variables are estimated as follows.

First, agglomeration of the secondary industry. The ratio between the share of the secondary industry in GDP of each province (or prefecture level city) and the share of the secondary industry in GDP of the whole country (the regional industrialization rate/the national industrialization rate) is used to measure the level of secondary industry agglomeration (or industrialization level). The sharing of infrastructure and the improvement of labor market matching (or job matching) efficiency driven by secondary industry agglomeration are both important factors in attracting FDI.

Second, total population. It refers to the total population of each province (or prefecture-level city) at the end of year (of which logarithm is then taken). The size of population is a good indicator of the market size of a region. When foreign capital invests in the service industry to tap the local market, population is the main factor of consideration. At the same time, the inclusion of the logarithm of total population in the model means that all variables are rendered into their per-capita forms, so that the econometric model is consistent with the theoretical model.

(5) Data sources

Provincial FDI data come from the database of China Entrepreneur Investment Club (CEIC), and other provincial data are derived from China Statistical Yearbooks. Average years of schooling for prefecture-level cities are based on the 2000 Population Census by County and the 2010 Population Census by County, and other data of prefecture-level cities are derived from China City Statistical Yearbooks.

Table 7.1 shows the explained variable, core explanatory variables and control variables.

7.3 Analysis of Estimation Results

7.3.1 *Impacts of Infrastructure on FDI Inflows: Evidence at the Provincial Level*

Table 7.2 shows the estimation results of the effects of social and economic infrastructure on FDI inflows at the provincial level. In order to avoid multicollinearity caused by the correlation of variables in social infrastructure, variables are examined one by one. Model (1), Model (3), Model (5), and Model (7) estimate of fixed effects, and Model (2), Model (4), Model (6), Model (8) estimate random effects. The F-test of the provincial fixed effectηi shows that the estimation results of fixed effects are significantly better than those produced by mixed OLS. The Hausman test further shows that the estimation results of fixed effects are significantly better than those of random effects. Therefore, the analysis of this research is mainly based on the estimation results of fixed effects. The estimation results are analyzed as follows.

First, in each model, the coefficient of the transportation infrastructure index is significantly positive, which means that the improvement of economic infrastructure is still an important factor in attracting FDI inflows. According to the estimation

Table 7.1 Basic Statistics

Provincial variables

Type		Variable	Unit	Observation	Average	Standard deviation	Minimum	Maximum
Explained variable		FDI (logarithm)	10,000 RMB yuan	577	13.785	1.839	8.243	16.932
Core explanatory variables	Social infrastructure	Density of university students	–	589	1.317	0.763	0.116	3.565
		Density of primary school teachers and students	–	403	601.708	116.892	377.074	1018.330
		Density of junior high school teachers and students	–	403	715.082	155.336	407.000	1246.883
		Density of senior high school teachers and students	–	403	655.373	134.616	431.406	1290.323
		Density of college teachers and students	–	403	587.503	48.353	516.529	926.784
		Teacher-student ratio	–	403	0.000	1.000	– 2.034	3.482
		Average years of schooling	Year	496	8.387	1.223	3.738	12.304
	Economical infrastructure	Road mileage per capita (logarithm)	km/10,000 people	589	3.163	0.740	1.301	5.518
		Railway mileage per capita (logarithm)	km/10,000 people	589	0.565	0.329	0.000	1.772
		Transportation Infrastructure Index	–	589	0.000	1.000	– 2.142	3.065

(continued)

Table 7.1 (continued)

Provincial variables								
Control variables		Agglomeration of the secondary industry	–	589	0.993	0.183	0.434	1.273
		Total population (logarithm)	10,000 people	589	8.063	0.869	5.529	9.306
Provincial variables								
Type		Variable	Unit	Observation	Average	Standard deviation	Minimum	Maximum
Explained variable		FDI (logarithm)	10,000 RMB yuan	4814	10.943	2.190	0.000	16.064
Core explanatory variables	Social infrastructure	Density of university students	–	4657	1.297	1.936	0.000	12.937
		Density of primary school teachers and students	–	4771	565.574	142.169	187.680	1975.625
		Density of high school teachers and students	–	4771	662.200	174.999	8.035	2274.085
		Density of college teachers and students	–	4538	672.007	366.135	121.383	7090.069
		Teacher-student ratio	–	4538	0.000	1.000	– 2.128	10.422
		Average years of schooling	Year	580	8.300	1.027	5.080	11.710
	Economical infrastructure	Road mileage per capita (logarithm)	km/10,000 people	4991	3.002	0.893	0.278	7.532
		Railway mileage per capita (logarithm)	km/10,000 people	4991	– 0.557	0.957	-3.977	3.660

(continued)

Table 7.1 (continued)

Provincial variables								
		transportation Infrastructure Index	–	4991	0.000	1.000	– 3.089	4.941
Control variables		Agglomeration of the secondary industry	–	4993	1.050	0.250	0.191	1.980
		Total population (logarithm)	10,000 people	5001	5.834	0.702	2.660	8.124

Note The time span of each variable is not exactly the same. Among the provincial variable, the variables related to the teacher-student ratio correspond to the data from 2004 to 2016, the average number of years of education corresponds to the data from 2001 to 2016, and the other variable correspond to the data from 1998 to 2016. Among the prefecture-level city variable, for the average years of education, only the census data of 2000 and 2010 are available, and all other variable correspond to the data from 1999 to 2015

Table 7.2 Infrastructure and FDI inflows—estimates based on provincial data

	Model1	Model 2	Model 3	Model 4	Model 5	Model 6	Model 7	Model 8
Explained variable	FDI (logarithm)							
The density of university/college students			0.4357*** [0.0870]	0.7448*** [0.0755]				
Teacher-student ratio					0.4579*** [0.0730]	0.6181*** [0.0599]		
Average years of schooling							0.3949*** [0.0913]	0.6501*** [0.0670]
transportation Infrastructure Index	1.2651*** [0.0758]	1.1556*** [0.0696]	0.8784*** [0.1071]	0.4494*** [0.0941]	0.4377*** [0.149]	– 0.0497 [0.1171]	0.8823*** [0.1188]	0.4768*** [0.0976]
Agglomeration of the secondary industry	1.4281*** [0.3271]	1.6387*** [0.3245]	1.1427*** [0.325 1]	1.3215*** [0.3069]	1.474 4*** [0.4093]	1.982 6*** [0.3855]	1.4397*** [0.3704]	1.6911*** [0.3492]
Total population (logarithm)	2.528 5*** [0.3737]	2.0947*** [0.1948]	1.6670*** [0.4041]	1.420 3*** [0.1807]	0.06719 [0.6583]	1.1893*** [0.1945]	1.5953*** [0.5806]	1.2159*** [0.2054]
Observation	577	577	577	577	399	399	489	489
Adjusted R^2	0.633 4	0.6320	0.6496	0.638 6	0.4655	0.446 2	0.5877	0.5764
F distribution/χ^2	312.6656	767.7242	251.1745	942.2823	79.2508	345.3524	161.8031	632.4248

(continued)

Table 7.2 (continued)

	Model1	Model 2	Model 3	Model 4	Model 5	Model 6	Model 7	Model 8
p-value	0.000 0	0.0000	0.0000	0.0000	0.0000	0.0000	0.0000	0.0000
F-test: $\eta_i = 0$	102.0648		44.9686		33.0021		43.1992	
Hausman test	84.07		72.94		36.32		19.96	
Estimation method	Fixed effects	Random effects	Fixed effects	Random effects	Fixed effects	Random effects	Fixed effects	Random effects

Notes
1. ***, **, * indicate the significance levels of 1%, 5%, and 10% respectively
2. The F distribution is suitable for fixed effects, and the χ^2 value is suitable for random effects
3. Values in [ ] are robust standard errors
4. The estimation results of the constant term are omitted from the table

results of Model (1), when other variables remain unchanged, for every 0.01 increase in the transportation infrastructure index, FDI inflows in a province will increase by 1.2651%. After human capital variables are added, however, the coefficient of the transportation infrastructure index declines significantly, from 1.2651 in Model (1) to below 1, which shows that the importance of economic infrastructure for attracting FDI inflows may be overestimated while social infrastructure is ignored.

Second, according to the estimation results of Model (3), Model (5) and Model (7), all variables under social infrastructure are significantly positive, which indicates that improving education and human capital is an effective means to promote FDI, but different social infrastructure variables have different effects. Given that other variables remain unchanged, FDI inflows into a province will increase by 0.4357% when the density of university/college students increases by 0.01. Similarly, every 0.01 increase in the teacher-student ratio, FDI inflows will increase by 0.4579%. When the average years of education increase by 0.1, FDI inflows will increase by 3.949%. The above estimation results show that foreign capital not only pays attention to the current level of average human capital of a province, but also pays attention to the level of quality human capital and the future level of human capital.

The estimation results of the control variables are also suggestive. First, the coefficient of the agglomeration of the secondary industry is always significantly positive. According to the estimation results of Model (3), while other variables remain unchanged, every 0.01 increase in the agglomeration of the secondary industry will raise FDI inflows into a province by 1.1427%. This may be because the agglomeration of the secondary industry creates the benefits of economies of scale, which not only dilutes the average construction cost of infrastructure, but also improves labor market matching efficiency.[3] Second, the total population is also significantly positive. According to the estimation result of Model (3), when the total population increases by 0.01, FDI inflows into a province will increase by 1.6670%, which means that population size has always been a factor that foreign capital values.

7.3.2 *Impacts of Infrastructure on FDI Inflows: Evidence at the City Level*

Table 7.3 shows the estimation results of the impact of social infrastructure and economic infrastructure on FDI inflows into prefecture-level cities. Model (9), Model (11), Model (13), and Model (15) estimate fixed effects, and Model (10), Model (12), Model (14), and Model (16) estimate random effects. The F-test of the fixed effect ηi also shows that the estimation results of fixed effects of prefecture-level cities are significantly better than those produced by mixed OLS. The Hausman test also shows that the estimation results of fixed effects are significantly better than those of random effects. Therefore, the analysis of this research is mainly based on the

[3] The agglomeration of the tertiary industry is also considered, but it is not significant, so it is not shown in the models. Relevant results are available upon request.

estimation results of fixed effects. Overall, the estimation results based on the data of prefecture-level cities and the estimation results based on provincial data are basically consistent in the direction and significance of coefficients. City-level data can help avoid the aggregation bias caused by the omission of differences between cities in provincial data. The estimation results are analyzed as follows.

First, before the inclusion of variables under social infrastructure, the coefficients of economic infrastructure variables are significantly positive. According to the estimation results of Model (9), when the transportation infrastructure index increases by 0.01, FDI inflows into a city will increase by 1.2739%. However, after human capital variables are added, the coefficient of the transportation infrastructure index declines significantly and becomes no longer significant in Model (15).

Second, variables under social infrastructure are also significantly positive, which is consistent with the results shown in Table 7.2, indicating that social infrastructure is an important factor in promoting FDI inflows. When other variables remain unchanged, when the density of university/college students increases by 0.01, FDI inflows into a city will increase by 0.1053%. Similarly, when the teacher-student ratio increases 0.01, FDI inflows into a city will increase by 0.2287%. When the average years of schooling increase by 0.1, FDI inflows into a city will increase by 721%. The above results show that the improvement of a city's social infrastructure, especially in the current level of average human capital, the level of quality human capital and the future level of human capital, is significant for attracting FDI inflows.

In order to avoid reverse causation between FDI and the variables, variables with a lag of one period are used to re-estimate each model. The re-estimation results of fixed effects are shown in Table 7.4. Correlation tests also show that the re-estimation results of fixed effects are significantly better than the results of mixed OLS and random effects. There is basic consistency between the estimation results of the benchmark models and the results of estimation using lagged variables in the scale, direction and significance of coefficients. Economic infrastructure still has a significant positive effect on FDI inflows, while social infrastructure is still a key factor in attracting FDI inflows. In a word, the conclusion based on the model estimation results is robust.

7.4 Key Findings and Policy Implications

Strengthening infrastructure development and giving full play to the role of human capital are two major tasks in China's supply-side structural reform (Chen 2017). Based on panel data of China's provinces and prefecture-level cities, this research explores the roles of social infrastructure and economic infrastructure in attracting FDI inflows. The study finds that foreign capital attaches importance to the availability and adequacy of social infrastructure in a target province or city, focusing on the current level of average human capital, the level of high-quality human capital, and the future level of human capital, while economic infrastructure is also a positive factor in promoting FDI.

Table 7.3 Infrastructure and FDI inflows—estimates based on prefectural-level city data

	Model 9	Model 10	Model 11	Model 12	Model 13	Model 14	Model 15	Model 16
Explained variable	FDI (logarithm)							
The density of university/college students			0.1053*** [0.0212]	0.1569*** [0.0198]				
Teacher-student ratio					0.2287*** [0. 030 1]	0.2662*** [0.0287]		
Average years of schooling							0.9721*** [0.2245]	1.4316*** [0.1087]
Transportation infrastructure index	1.2739*** [0.0532]	1.1316*** [0.0486]	1.1228*** [0.0631]	0.8541*** [0.0571]	0.9721*** [0.062 8]	0.8147*** [0.0557]	0.3183*** [0.3183]	0.5021*** [0.1265]
Agglomeration of the secondary industry	1.2044*** [0.1504]	1.3847*** [0.1431]	1.3274*** [0.1617]	1.6300*** [0.1504]	0.9184*** [0.1531]	1.0913*** [0.1451]	1.2596*** [0.6547]	1.0429*** [0.3968]
Total population (logarithm)	2.2225*** [0.1967]	2.2907*** [0.1201]	1.9237 *** [0.2330]	2.0011 *** [0.1197]	2.0297 *** [0.2154]	1.9941*** [0.1226]	− 0.5211 [1.0359]	1.1243*** [0.1614]
Observation	4802	4802	451 2	4512	4393	4393	536	536
Adjusted R^2	0.2593	0.2586	0.259 4	0.2563	0.2672	0.2662	0.4524	0.4247
F distribution/χ^2	526.3273	1616.6266	369.5542	1547.4246	373.943	1 547.6552	52.0467	381.5132
P-value	0.0000	0.0000	0.0000	0.0000	0.0000	0.0000	0.0000	0.0000
F-test: $\eta_i = 0$	38.2392		28.3676		36.4184		2.8461	

(continued)

Table 7.3 (continued)

	Model 9	Model 10	Model 11	Model 12	Model 13	Model 14	Model 15	Model 16
Hausman test	60.29		141.73		35.17		18.50	
Estimation method	Fixed effects	Random effects	Fixed effects	Random effects	Fixed effects	Random effects	Fixed effects	Random effects

Note:
1. ***, **, * indicate the significance levels of 1%, 5%, and 10% respectively.
2. The F distribution is suitable for fixed effects, and the χ^2 value is suitable for random effects.
3. Values in [ ] are robust standard errors.
4. The estimation results of the constant term are omitted from the table.

Table 7.4 Infrastructure and FDI inflows: estimation results using lagged variables

	Model 17	Model 18	Model 19	Model 20	Model 21	Model 22	Model 23	Model 24
Explained variable	FDI (logarithm)							
The density of university/ college students × (t − 1)		0.6266*** [0.0866]				0.0964*** [0.0202]		
Teacher-student ratio × (t − 1)			0.3825*** [0.069 7]				0.1728*** [0.0300]	
Average years of schooling × (t − 1)				0.433 7*** [0.0916]				1.0465*** [0.2057]
transportation Infrastructure Index × (t − 1)	1.2349*** [0.0827]	0.7071 *** [0.1074]	0.3729*** [0.1301]	0.7734*** [0.1190]	1.1571*** [0.0552]	1.0208*** [0.0597]	0.9349*** [0.0610]	− 0.0756 [0.2914]
Agglomeration of the secondary industry × (t − 1)	1.4939*** [0.3619]	1.0059*** [0.3516]	0.9342*** [0.4178]	1.2708*** [0.4124]	1.1954*** [0.1582]	1.0742*** [0.1559]	0.7240*** [0.1534]	1.5753*** [0.6067]
Total population (logarithm) × (t − 1)	2.5016*** [0.4014]	1.1635*** [0.4250]	0.3201 *** [0.6419]	1.132 9 *** [0.6100]	2.4911*** [0.2063]	2.0031*** [0.2201]	2.1217***[0.2110]	− 0.1002*** [0.955 7]
Observation	548	548	369	459	4527	422 7	4116	534
Adjusted R^2	0.6113	0.6473	0.3909	0.5401	0.2344	0.2495	0.2430	0.4541
*F*value	269.4596	235.3998	53.5906	124.4799	432.3349	327.0152	306.9497	52.4133
P-value	0.0000	0.0000	0.0000	0.0000	0.0000	0.0000	0.0000	0.0000
Estimation method	Fixed effects of provincial data				Fixed effects of prefecture-level city data			

Note

1. ***, **, * indicate the significance levels of 1%, 5%, and 10% respectively
2. Values in [ ] are robust standard errors
3. The estimation results of the constant term are omitted from the table

This study has significant theoretical and practical implications. It gives insights into how FDI in China is affected by the sluggish global economic recovery and China's economic transformation and how foreign capital selects investment destinations, especially the effects of social infrastructure, in this context. It therefore informs the formulation and adjustment of infrastructure-related public policies and helps create a favorable investment environment to boost comprehensive opening-up. At the same time, this research supports research on the economic effects of infrastructure in developing countries.

The policy implications of its findings are as follows.

First, China's provincial and municipal governments should pay close attention to the key role of social infrastructure in attracting FDI inflows, and actively improve the level of human capital in their province or city. The Report to the 19th National Congress of the CPC emphasizes the strategy of developing a quality workforce, pointing out that "people with talent are a strategic resource for China as it endeavors to achieve national rejuvenation and stay ahead in international competition." A higher level of human capital can not only improve the return on capital of multinational companies, but also give provinces or cities a higher "absorptive capacity", thereby helping them attract more FDI in technology-intensive and high added value projects. According to the empirical research results of this research, investment should be further increased in higher education, and the level of quality human capital of a province or city should be raised by gradually increasing the proportion of the population with higher education. Meanwhile, teachers should be given better working conditions, including higher pays, which would attract more teachers and raise the ratio of teachers to students, and thus help improve educational resource provision in both scale and quality and lay a foundation for raising the level of human capital in a province or city.

Second, the role of economic infrastructure in attracting FDI inflows should be considered reasonably, and the mode of economic infrastructure provision should be optimized while construction expands. Economic infrastructure, which has some attributes of public goods, is a basic condition for improving the quality of provision, and plays an important role in the development of national economy. Better transportation infrastructure can significantly reduce transportation costs, thereby increasing the return on capital of multinational corporations. According to the empirical research results of this research, transportation infrastructure is still a positive factor in attracting FDI inflows. Therefore, the construction of transportation infrastructure should be expanded to improve inter-connectivity, which is a policy tool to attract FDI inflows in the future. At the same time, it is also necessary to be aware of some shortcomings in the current mode of infrastructure provision, especially the dependence on debt financing which may exacerbate the financial risk in regions with inadequate financial resources in the context of China's economic slowdown. Therefore, this research believes that it is necessary to update the model of infrastructure financing, increase the ratio of central government expenditure in infrastructure construction, and thus make infrastructure really a public good.

While this research uses both the data of provinces and prefecture-level cities in its empirical research, and has obtained robust empirical results, there are still limitations. First, since there are multiple factors affecting FDI inflows, and some of them are difficult to measure (such as business environment and government efficiency), omitted-variable bias (OVB) is inevitable. Second, while it examines the effects of economic infrastructure and social infrastructure on FDI inflows from an empirical perspective, this research may have failed to identify mechanisms by which they affect FDI inflows. Finally, due to differences in development levels and institutional arrangements, the applicability of the policy recommendations of this research to provinces and cities remains a question which should be answered through further research.

References

Ansar, A., Fluvbjerg, B., Budzier, A.: Does infrastructure investment lead to economic growth or economic fragility? Evidence from China. Oxf. Rev. Econ. Policy. Rev. Econ. Policy **32**(3), 360–390 (2016)

Chen, H.: Deeping the Supply-side Structural Reform. Coaching Reader of the Report to the 19th National Congress of the CPC. People's Publishing House, Beijing (2017)

De Gregorio, J., Lee, J.W.: How does foreign direct investment affect economic Growth? J. Int. Econ. **45**(1), 115–135 (1998)

Fu, Y., Zhang, Y.: Chinese decentralization and fiscal expenditure bias: the costs of competing for growth. Management World **3**, 4–12, 22 (2007)

Lucas, R.E.: Why doesn't capital flow from rich to poor countries? Am. Econ. Rev. **80**(2), 92–96 (1990)

Shi, H., Huang, S.: How much infrastructure is too much? A new approach and evidence from China. World Dev. **56**, 272–286 (2014)

Wu, W., Zhang, L.: Does fiscal investment in education affect the location selection of FDI? An empirical study from the perspective of human capital mobility. Educ. Econ. **1**, 48–58 (2017)

Zhang, J., Gao, Y., Fu, Y.: Why does China have good infrastructure?" Econ. Res. J. **3**, 4–19 (2007)

Chapter 8
Infrastructure's Influence on People's Well-Being: Taking Access to Natural Gas as an Example

Everything we do aims to ensure that the people live a happier life with more dignity.
—Wen Jiabao, Report on the Work of the Government (2010)

This chapter discusses the impacts of clean-fuel infrastructure on people's well-being, or the level of happiness, taking access to natural gas as an example. The chapter compares the statistics from Chinese General Social Survey (CGSS) with the macroeconomic data of China's provinces, and estimates people's level of well-being quantitatively using OLS and Ordered Probit models. This research finds that natural gas accessibility significantly improves people's well-being. Further analysis shows that it has a more obvious effect on people in areas with high industrial emissions. This chapter not only explains the factors affecting the well-being of Chinese people, but also informs policies concerning clean-fuel infrastructure development.

8.1 Motivation

8.1.1 Clean Fuel and People's Well-Being

Improving the people's livelihood and well-being is an important goal of social and economic development in any country. As the Report to the 19th National Congress of the CPC points out, "The original aspiration and the mission of Chinese Communists is to seek happiness for the Chinese people and rejuvenation for the Chinese nation." Continuous efforts are needed to "meet people's ever-growing needs for a better life" to ensure that "our people will always have a strong sense of fulfillment, happiness, and security." In recent years, facing economic slowdown and the economic shift, Chinese government has regarded "shoring up weak links in areas that are important to people's lives" as one of the main tasks in deepening the supply-side structural reform. In September 2019, the State Council issued a circular entitled "Seeking Happiness for People: 70 Years of Progress on Human Rights in China" which stresses that "living a happy life is the primary human right".

C. Pan, *Urban Infrastructure and Economic Development in China*, Public Economy and Urban Governance in China, https://doi.org/10.1007/978-981-99-6629-5_8

For a long time, scholars have tried to explain factors behind happiness and public policies to make people happier in China, and produced a series of enlightening research outcomes. Empirical studies have found that among all the factors affecting Chinese people' happiness, some are common in all countries, such as gender, age, marital status, employment, place of residence, and religion, while others are specific to China's current economic development stage, such as inequality of opportunities, the household registration system, housing prices, and environmental pollution (Pan 2019).

Despite these findings, the positive impact of the access to clean fuel on people's well-being has not been thoroughly investigated. Since the early twenty-first century, the rapid increase in the supply and widespread use of clean fuel, including natural gas, has disrupted China's traditional coal-based energy mix. At the same time, since natural gas is clean and safe, its popularity not only helps improve air quality, but also benefits the lives of millions of households.

Figure 8.1 shows the share of natural gas in total energy consumption and the subjective well-being, or happy feeling, of Chinese people. (Refer to Section 8.3 for details on the measurement of people's subjective well-being.) The share of natural gas is measured by the proportion of natural gas to total energy consumed (coal, oil, natural gas, hydropower, nuclear power, wind power, etc.). From 2000 to 2018, the index of people's subjective well-being continued to rise, up from 3.27 in 2003 to 3.90 in 2011, followed by a decline and then climbing back to 3.87 in 2015. Meanwhile, the share of natural gas in China continued to rise, up from 2.20% in 2000 to 7.80% in 2018. During this period, total natural gas consumption[1] grew by 14.4% annually, much higher than China's economic growth over the same period.

8.1.2 Research Questions

The positive correlation between natural gas consumption and people's subjective well-being in Figure 8.1 raises an important question: does the widespread use of natural gas improve people's well-being? In other words, is there a causal relationship between "natural gas" and "well-being"? If the answer is yes, what exactly contributes to this relationship?

To answer these questions, an equation is designed for measuring people's well-being using OLS and Ordered Probit models with statistics from the Chinese General Social Survey (CGSS) for five years (2010, 2011, 2012, 2013, 2015) and the macroeconomic data of China's provinces. It is found that access to natural gas has significantly increased people's well-being. Further analysis shows that this effect is more pronounced in areas with higher industrial emissions.

Clearly, the correlation between natural gas and people's well-being has important theoretical and policy implications. First, it helps explain the factors affecting

[1] The average annual growth rate in this chapter is calculated in the same way as in Chap. 5.

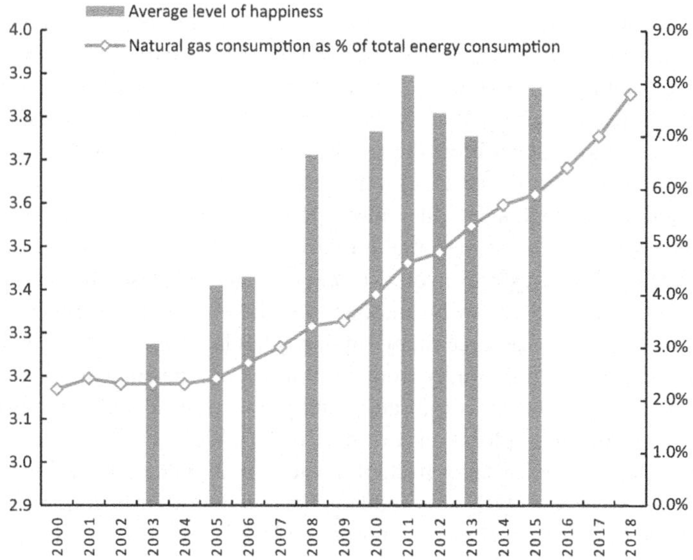

Fig. 8.1 Share of natural gas in total energy consumption and people's subjective well-being in China. *Source* Chinese General Social Survey and China Statistical Yearbooks

people's well-being at the current stage of China's economic development, especially the role of improving clean-fuel infrastructure including natural gas in raising people's level of happiness. Second, it is a basis for developing policies related to clean-fuel infrastructure development. In addition, it is well aligned with studies on the socio-economic effects of energy infrastructure in developing countries.

It is worth noting that no study on the impact of access to natural gas on people's well-being in China has been conducted so far, and this research is dedicated to filling this gap.

8.2 History of Natural Gas in China

Natural gas is a mixture of various gases, mainly gaseous hydrocarbons, produced through the biochemical decomposition of organic matter. It is found either in fractures and cavities in rocks with oil or in groundwater in a dissolved state. Mainly composed of methane (85–95%), ethane, propane, butane, it is a high-quality fuel and chemical material.[2]

Natural gas is a safe, clean, and efficient energy source. First, it is colorless, odorless, non-toxic, non-corrosive, and lighter than air. Therefore, in case it leaks, it will move upward and dissipate in the air, causing no explosion. Second, since

[2] Source: Statistics Report on Energy 2019, NBS.

natural gas contains almost no sulfur or dust, substituting natural gas for coal and oil significantly reduces emissions of pollutants such as particles, carbon dioxide, sulfur dioxide, and nitrogen oxides, and thus helps curb acid rain and the greenhouse effect, improving atmospheric quality. Third, natural gas has a high calorific value, as burning natural gas produces more than twice the heat from burning the same amount of manufactured gas. For these reasons, the substitution of clean fuels such as natural gas for traditional fuels that produce more pollutants is a major move in updating China's energy policy and an essential initiative to realize sustainable development.

Since 1949, China has endeavored to explore natural gas resources within its territory, mainly in the Sichuan Basin, the Ordos Basin, the Tarim Basin, as well as coastal areas, and has discovered many small gas fields. From 1949 to 1975, China's natural gas production rose rapidly from 7 million cubic meters to 8.85 billion cubic meters. After that, natural gas exploration and production slowed down in China as it focused more on oil exploration. From 1976 to 2000, China's domestic natural gas production increased weakly from 10 billion cubic meters to 27.2 billion cubic meters. However, since 2001, this industry has shown a strong momentum after large-scale energy projects began including the West–East natural gas pipeline and the Sichuan-East natural gas pipeline. Four major natural gas production bases have been built up in the Ordos Basin, the Tarim Basin, the Sichuan Basin and South China Sea (Zhu 2019).

The Report to the 19th National Congress of the CPC emphasized the need to "promote a revolution in energy production and consumption, and build an energy sector that is clean, low-carbon, safe, and efficient." In 2018, China's State Council issued *Opinions on Promoting the Coordinated and Stable Development of Natural Gas*, which gives guidelines on how to reshape the industry in 10 aspects (exploration and development, diversified supply, reserves, infrastructure, supply and demand forecasting, comprehensive coordination, demand management, emergency response, pricing mechanism, and safe operation) in order to create a framework for future natural gas development in China.

In this context, China has accelerated the building of natural gas production, supply, storage, and marketing systems, strengthening top-down policy guidance, intensifying exploration and exploitation efforts, and improving infrastructure in key regions. As a result, the natural gas industry in China has made successive breakthroughs. In 2018, natural gas consumption reached 280.3 billion cubic meters, 7.8% of total primary energy consumption in China, and natural gas consumption has increased significantly in all provinces. At the same time, natural gas infrastructure has improved steadily. By the end of 2018, the total mileage of natural gas pipelines in China reached 76,000 kilometers, creating a gas transmission capacity of 320 billion cubic meters per year.[3]

Figure 8.2 shows China's natural gas production and economic growth since its reform and opening-up program began, in which natural gas production[4] includes gas

[3] Source: China Natural Gas Development Report 2019.

[4] Equation: Natural gas production = sales volume + enterprises' own gas consumption + losses and transmission difference + closing stock—opening stock.

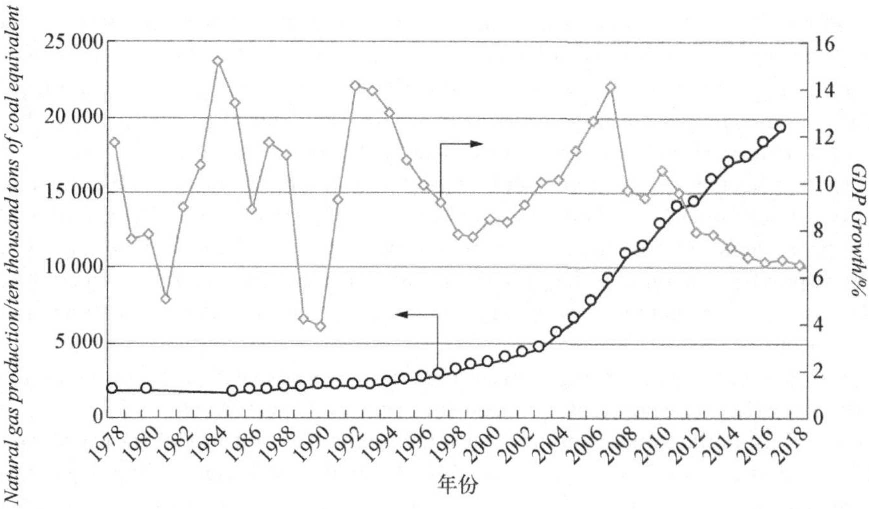

Fig. 8.2 China's natural gas production and economic growth since reform and opening−up. *Source* China Statistical Yearbooks

transmitted and used locally. First, from 1978 to 2017, China's natural gas production increased from 18.2 million tons of coal equivalent to 193.59 million tons of coal equivalent, with an average annual growth of 7.88%, a clear evidence of China's remarkable achievement in natural gas. Second, on the development curve, China's natural gas production can be divided into two phases: the first phase (1985–2001) saw the production growing at an average annual rate of 5.42%, while during the second phase (2001–2017), the average annual growth rate reached 10.71%. That means China's natural gas production accelerated after 2001 and the momentum of fast growth has continued over the last decade though China's economy slowed down.

8.3 Empirical Research Methodology

8.3.1 Equations to Estimate People's Level of Happiness

The following equation is designed to estimate the impact of access to natural gas on people's level of happiness quantitatively:

$$Happy_{ipt} = \alpha lnY_{ipt} + \beta ln(NGAS)_{pt} + \gamma M_{ipt} + \delta N_{pt} + \theta_t + \mu_p + \varepsilon_{ipt} \quad (8.1)$$

In which, i is the respondent; p the province where the respondent lives; t is the year; $Happy_{ipt}$ is the level of happiness (or subjective well-being) of the respondent; lnY is the respondent's income (logarithm); $ln(NGAS)_{pt}$ is the natural gas consumption per capita in province p in year t, reflecting the scale of clean fuel infrastructure; M and N are the individual-level and provincial-level control variables (see Sect. 8.3.3 for more details about these variables); θ_t and μ_p are the fixed effect of year and the fixed effects of province; ε is the error term; $\alpha, \beta, \gamma, and\, \delta$ are the parameters to be estimated, in which α measures the effect of income level on the respondent's happiness and β measures the effect of clean-fuel infrastructure on the respondent's happiness, both being the focus of this research. It is assumed that $\alpha > 0$ and $\beta > 0$.

Since subjective well-being is an Ordered Probit variable with uneven quantitative differences between adjacent options, using OLS to make estimations may result in errors, thus similar studies prefer to use the Ordered Probit model for estimation. However, it is also found that concerning the explained variables, the estimation results obtained by using the OLS model and the Ordered Probit model are consistent in terms of direction and significance of coefficients, and the OLS estimation results can better explain the economic meaning of coefficients. Therefore, this research presents the estimation results of both OLS and Ordered Probit models, but analysis is mainly based on the OLS results.

8.3.2 Theoretical Analysis and Model Setting

To quantify the respondent's marginal willingness to pay for clean fuel, the full differentiation of above variables is made 0:

$$dHappy = (\partial Happy/\partial NGAS) \cdot dNGAS + (\partial H/\partial Y) \cdot dY = 0 \tag{8.2}$$

Therefore, the respondent's marginal willingness to pay for natural gas is:

$$MWTP \equiv dY/dNGAS = -(\beta/\alpha) \cdot (Y/NGAS) \tag{8.3}$$

An obvious interpretation of Eq. (8.3) is that individuals are willing to pay a certain sum of money ($MWTP$) to increase the use of natural gas, thus keeping the level of utility (happiness) unchanged. Given that $MWTP$ varies with Y and NGAS, their sample means are substituted for both variables to measure the average marginal willingness to pay ($AMWTP$):

$$AMWTP = -(\beta/\alpha) \cdot \left(\overline{Y}/\overline{NGAS}\right) \tag{8.4}$$

8.3.2.1 Variable Construction and Data Sources

(1) Explained variable: Subjective well-being (level of happiness)

Subjective well-being is the explained variable of this research. In the CGSS of each year, the respondent's subjective evaluation of his or her life was investigated. Although the questions and the order of alternatives for the happiness survey are different in different years, the respondent's happiness was always classified into 5 levels from low to high: "very unhappy", "unhappy", "average", "happy", "very happy", which are sequentially assigned as 1, 2, 3, 4, and 5. So, an Ordered Probit variable is constructed to measure the level of happiness.

(2) Core explanatory variable: Natural gas penetration

Natural gas penetration is the core explanatory variable of this research, measured by the logarithm of natural gas consumption per capita in each province (in m3/person), which also reflects the scale of the natural gas infrastructure.

(3) Individual-level control variables

In order to minimize the estimation bias due to any potential omission of variable(s), the following individual-level control variables are used for the empirical study of happiness.

First, income level, measured as the logarithm of the respondent's annual personal income.

Second, gender, defined as: "male" = 1, "female" = 0.

Third, age, measured by the square value of age (divided by 1,000).

Fourth, education level, measured by the minimum time the respondent has spent to obtain a degree, with "illiterate" being the lowest value (0) and "postgraduate" being the highest (19).

Fifth, self-rated health, measured by respondent's subjective assessment of his or her own health status. Like happiness, the estimated health is divided into 5 levels: "very poor" = 1, "poor" = 2, "fair" = 3, "good" = 4, and "very good" = 5.

Sixth, household register, defined as "registered urban residence" = 1; "registered rural residence" = 0.

Seventh, marital status, defined as "married" = 1; "unmarried or divorced" = 0.

Eighth, unemployment, defined as "unemployed" = 1; "employed full time or part time" = 0.

(4) Provincial-level control variables

The following provincial-level control variables are used as well.

First, the level of industrialization, measured by the ratio of industrial output to GDP in the province where the respondent lives. The level of industrialization of a region not only affects the demand for energy in that region, but also has an impact on the well-being of local people.

Second, the level of openness, measured by the ratio of total imports and exports to GDP in the province where the respondent lives. The openness of a region may be directly related to the import of natural gas and may also have an impact on the well-being of local people (Ma and Cai 2014).

Third, emissions per unit of industrial output (logarithm), measured as the logarithm of sulfur dioxide emissions per unit of industrial output in the province where the respondent lives, which reflects the industrial emissions and pollution levels in a region. This variable is used to examine the differential impact of clean fuel penetration on people's well-being in regions with different levels of industrial pollution and emissions.

(5) Data sources

The data used in this research mainly come from two sources. The first is the CGSS of five years (2010, 2011, 2012, 2013, and 2015), which provides microscopic information on the respondent's subjective well-being, annual personal income, and demographic factors. As the surveys cover 31 provinces, autonomous regions and municipalities of China, this source contains more than 50,000 valid samples which are typical of China, and the same sampling method used in all five surveys also ensures the comparability of samples. The second source is the China Statistical Yearbooks of the same five years, which contain the macroscopic data of natural gas consumption and production in each province. Computing and comparing these data across years and provinces leads to the intertemporal and cross-sectional data derived from a total of 45,697 samples.

The above-mentioned explained variables, core explanatory variables, and control variables are shown in Table 8.1. Emissions per unit of industrial output are not included in the table as they are only used as a coordinating variable.

8.4 Analysis of Estimation Results

8.4.1 Effect of Natural Gas Penetration on Happiness

Table 8.2 shows the results of equations to measure people's well-being using different variables. In this table, Models 1 to 3 use OLS; Model 1 does not use the fixed effects of province or year while Model 2 does and Model 3 also uses provincial-level control variables (levels of industrialization and openness); and Model 4 computes a maximum likelihood estimation using the Ordered Probit model. Each model is highly significant, while compared to Models 3 and 4, the other models have estimated coefficients which show highly consistent direction and significance, so analysis is based on Model 3.

Table 8.2 shows that the coefficient of the core explanatory variable "natural gas penetration" is significantly positive, representing that the subjective well-being of people is higher in areas with higher natural gas penetration. If a series of individual-level and provincial-level controlled variables are used to reduce errors in estimation, this correlation can be interpreted as a causal effect, indicating that the popularity of

Table. 8.1 Basic statistics

Variables	Observation	Average	Standard deviation	Minimum	Maximum
Subjective well-being	45,697	3.8181	0.8474	1	5
Natural gas consumption per capita (logarithm)	45,697	0.0129	0.0126	0.0004	0.0728
Annual personal income (logarithm)	45,697	9.2643	1.2869	7.3132	13.7747
Gender: Male	45,697	0.4971	0.5000	0	1
Age	45,697	48.9676	15.9253	17	102
The square of age/1000	45,697	2.6514	1.6205	0.2890	10.4040
Education level	45,697	8.7233	4.6029	0	19
Self-assessment of health	45 697	3.5301	1.1271	1	5
Urban residence registration	45,697	0.4202	0.4936	0	1
Marital Status: Married	45,697	0.8073	0.3944	0	1
Unemployment	45,697	0.3178	0.4656	0	1
Level of industrialization	45,697	0.4744	0.0787	0.1974	0.5905
Level of openness	45,697	0.3056	0.3277	0.0152	1.4574

natural gas as a clean fuel raises the happiness of local people. The estimation results of Model 3 show that for every 1% increase in natural gas consumption per capita, people's subjective well-being will go up 3.9615%.

8.4.2 *Average Marginal Willingness to Pay*

Personal income has a positive effect on people's happiness, which has been confirmed by many empirical studies on happiness. According to the estimation results of Model 3, on average, for every 10% increase in annual personal income, people's subjective well-being will rise by 0.527%. However, it is worth adding that this gain is minimal, equivalent to 1.4‰ of average happiness of the samples (0.527%/3.8181), suggesting that although income is a positive factor behind people happiness, the effect of income growth on happiness is not significant. This also implies that as a country's economy grows and national income increases, the improvement in happiness may lag far behind the rise in income, which is an Easterlin Paradox. Therefore, in order to improve the subjective well-being of its population, a country should develop public policies that go beyond income.

More importantly, based on the above estimation results, the average marginal willingness to pay can be estimated. On average, consumers are willing to pay 12,981

Table 8.2 Estimation results of the impact of natural gas penetration on people's happiness

	Model 1	Model 2	Model 3	Model 4
Explained variables	Subjective well-being			
Natural gas consumption per capita (logarithm)	1.5048*** [0.3173]	3.0961** [1.2189]	3.9615*** [1.3302]	7.5717*** [1.9483]
Annual personal income (logarithm)	0.0458*** [0.0037]	0.0527*** [0.0038]	0.0527*** [0.0038]	0.0690*** [0.0054]
Gender: Male	− 0.1136*** [0.0081]	− 0.1174*** [0.0081]	− 0.1174*** [0.0081]	− 0.1641*** [0.0111]
Age	− 0.0321*** [0.0016]	− 0.0306*** [0.0016]	− 0.0306*** [0.0016]	− 0.0420*** [0.0022]
The square of age/1000	0.3828*** [0.0158]	0.3748*** [0.0157]	0.3749*** [0.0157]	0.5164*** [0.0220]
Education level	0.0121*** [0.0012]	0.0137*** [0.0012]	0.0136*** [0.0012]	0.0170*** [0.0017]
Self-assessment of health	0.1674*** [0.0041]	0.1833*** [0.0043]	0.1833*** [0.0043]	0.2505*** [0.0058]
Urban residence registration	− 0.0432*** [0.0095]	− 0.0235** [0.0097]	− 0.0235** [0.0097]	− 0.0281** [0.0135]
Marital status: Married	0.2799*** [0.0119]	0.2676*** [0.0119]	0.2677*** [0.0119]	0.3440*** [0.0155]
unemployment	− 0.0108 [0.0100]	[0.0049] 0.0100	[0.0047] 0.0100	[0.0195] 0.0136
Level of industrialization			− 0.0481 [0.2310]	− 0.2472 [0.3185]
Level of openness			0.1444* [0.0877]	0.2223* [0.1218]
Fixed effect of province	No	Yes	Yes	Yes
Fixed effect of year	No	Yes	Yes	Yes
Observation	45,697	45,697	45,697	45,697
Adjusted R^2/Pseudo R^2	0.0838	0.1108	0.1108	0.0514
F distribution/chi-square value	332.2789	351.4417	293.0838	4751.4638
p-value	0.0000	0.0000	0.0000	0.0000
Estimation method		OLS		Ordered Probit

Notes

***, **, and * stand for the significance levels of 1%, 5%, and 10% respectively.

F distribution is suitable for OLS estimation, while chi-squared value is suitable for Ordered Probit estimation.

Adjusted R^2 is suitable for OLS estimation, while dummy R2 is suitable for Ordered Probit estimation.

Values in [ ] are robust standard errors.

Estimation results of constant terms are omitted from the table.

RMB yuan to increase natural gas penetration by 1 cubic meter per 10,000 people, which implies a more positive consumer perception of natural gas.

The estimated coefficients of the control variables are enlightening. Given the key factors of individual income level and the fixed effect of year and province, the following conclusions can be drawn:

First, in terms of gender, men's happiness level is considerably lower than that of women. This may be because men are under more pressure in all aspects of life. Men's primary responsibility for buying a house, getting married, and supporting the family can lead to lower happiness.

Second, in terms of age, there is a significant U-shaped relationship between age and subjective well-being. The young and the elderly have relatively higher levels of well-being than middle-aged people, and according to the estimation of Model 3, happiness bottoms out at around age 41. Pressure from work, supporting the family and physical decline are the major factors behind the "midlife crisis".

Third, in terms of education background, a higher level of education raises happiness. This is because better education creates more opportunities for personal development and helps improve social status, and well-educated people pay more attention to the quality of life.

Fourth, in terms of health, self-rated health and subjective well-being are positively correlated. That means people who are or believe they are healthy have a higher sense of happiness. This is because better health helps improve work efficiency and quality of life, while an optimistic view of one's own health status may also raise the happiness level. In short, health and happiness are mutually reinforcing.

Fifth, in terms of household registration, the happiness of urban residents is notably lower than rural residents. While rapid urbanization has provided urban residents with better infrastructure and doing-business environment on the one hand, urban ills such as traffic congestion, high housing prices and environmental pollution have reduced their happiness on the other.

Sixth, in terms of marital status, being married contributes to happiness, which is consistent with the results of existing studies.

Seventh, in terms of employment status, unemployment does not lower people's happiness. This may be because although unemployed individuals temporarily lose a stable source of income, thanks to the steady improvement of the social security system and government support for re-employment, unemployment does not worsen individuals' expectations of their future and thus does not seriously impair happiness.

Eighth, in terms of industrialization, the level of regional industrialization is not a significant factor for people's happiness. While industrialization brings more opportunities for employment and business start-up, it also leads to negative externalities such as environmental pollution and traffic congestion. Given all these positive and negative factors, the association is weak between the level of regional industrialization and people's happiness.

Ninth, in terms of openness, a higher degree of trade openness in a region contributes to the well-being of its residents. This is because opening to the outside world fuels the growth of export-oriented enterprises, which in turn creates more jobs and development opportunities for workers. However, it must not be ignored that as the degree of openness increases, the impact of external fluctuations on the domestic economy becomes greater, which may lead to more uncertainties in employment, especially in the export sector, and thus negatively affect happiness.

8.4.3 Interaction Between Industrial Emissions and Natural Gas Penetration

Interaction between two variables: regional industrial emissions and natural gas penetration is also included in the model to investigate the heterogeneous effect of using clean fuel on people's well-being in regions with different pollution levels. Table 8.3 shows the results of the equation using OLS to measure people's happiness. First, the coefficient of the core explanatory variable "natural gas penetration" remains significantly positive, which is consistent with the findings presented in Sect. 8.4.1. Second, the coefficient of the variable "emissions per unit of industrial output" is significantly negative, indicating that higher industrial emissions noticeably reduce the happiness of local people, which is consistent with the finding of existing studies that pollution impairs the well-being and health of the local population. More importantly, the coefficient of the interaction between these two variables is significantly positive, which means that access to natural gas has a more obvious effect on the happiness of residents in areas with higher levels of industrial emissions, or in other words, the use of clean fuel reduces the negative impact of industrial emissions on the happiness of residents. It may be because in areas with higher levels of industrial pollution, people have higher expectations of the pollution-reducing effect of clean fuel, and therefore people's happiness increases with the penetration of natural gas.

8.5 Key Findings and Policy Implications

Revolutionizing energy production and consumption and shifting to a clean, low-carbon, safe and efficient energy system are key strategic initiatives to drive China's "green development". This chapter investigates the impact of clean-fuel infrastructure on people's well-being, taking access to natural gas as an example. Comparing the statistics from CGSS with China's provincial macroeconomic data, and estimating people's level of well-being quantitatively using OLS and Ordered Probit models, this chapter has three major findings as follows.

First, access to natural gas significantly improves people's well-being. Second, in terms of average marginal willingness to pay, consumers give a higher rating for the use of natural gas. Third, access to natural gas has a more significant effect on the happiness of people in areas with higher levels of industrial emissions. Different measurements of core explanatory variables or migration factors do not influence the above three findings.

Table 8.3 Estimation results of the interaction between industrial emissions and natural gas penetration

	Model 5	Model 6
Explained variables	Subjective well-being	
Natural gas consumption per capita (logarithm)	6.2938*** [1.5869]	6.5102*** [1. 6226]
ln*NGAS* × [Emissions per unit of industrial output (logarithm)]	3. 3381*** [1. 978]	3.2166*** [1.2219]
Natural gas consumption per capita (logarithm)	− 0.0487** [0.0231]	− 0.0438* [0. 0252]
Annual personal income (logarithm)	0.0529*** [0. 0038]	0.0529*** [0. 0038]
Gender: Male	− 0.1171*** [0.0081]	− 0.1171*** [0. 0081]
Age	− 0.0306*** [0. 0016]	− 0.0306*** [0.0016]
Square of age/1000	0.3749*** [0. 0157]	0.3749*** [0. 0157]
Education level	0.0136*** [0. 0012]	0.0136*** [0. 0012]
Self-assessment of health	0.1833*** [0.0043]	0.1833*** [0.0042]
Urban residence registration	− 0.0237** [0.0097]	− 0.0237** [0.0097]
Marital Status: Married	0.2679*** [0.0119]	0.2679*** [0.0119]
Unemployment	[0.005] 0.0100	[0.005] 0.0100
Level of industrialization		− 0.0271 [0.2398]
Level of openness		[0.0648] 0.0945
Fixed effect of province	Yes	Yes
Fixed effect of year fixed	Yes	Yes
Observation	45,697	45,697
Adjusted R^2	0.1110	0.1109
F distribution	293.3946	251.5875
p-value	0.0000	0.0000
Estimation method	OLS	

Notes
***, **, and * stand for the significance levels of 1%, 5%, and 10% respectively.
Values in [] are robust standard errors.
Estimation results of constant terms are omitted from the table.

The research presented in this chapter has high theoretical and policy relevance. Theoretically, this chapter explains the factors behind the well-being of Chinese people, focusing on clean fuel consumption and its positive effect. It also supplements empirical studies on the determinants of people's well-being in developing countries. Practically, this chapter informs policies related to clean-fuel infrastructure development in three ways.

First, the supply capacity of natural gas should be expanded to improve natural gas accessibility and popularity. On the premise of keeping ecological balance, China should further reform its natural gas exploration and exploitation system, and invest more money and efforts in domestic exploration to expand domestic natural gas supply. At the same time, China should accelerate the diversification of overseas natural gas sources in order to ensure long-term, stable overseas supply of natural gas, as well as diversifying transportation modes, import channels and contract types.

Second, natural gas infrastructure should be built more widely and interconnected more closely. China should accelerate the construction of natural gas pipelines and liquefied natural gas (LNG) receiving stations, and focus on major projects of pipeline inter-connectivity. Besides, to meet the growing market demand, China also should accelerate the development of coastal and inland LNG shipping, and release favorable policies to support multi-modal transportation of LNG. By improving the construction and inter-connectivity of natural gas infrastructure, clean fuel will benefit more people in more regions.

Third, natural gas and other clean fuels should be used scientifically to upgrade China's energy structure. China should establish a coordination mechanism for natural gas development and encourage the execution of annual, mid-term and long-term sales contracts for the sale and purchase of natural gas. At the same time, China should reasonably allocate electricity, gas, coal, oil, and other energy sources according to the local situation, and make full use of clean fuels to reform the energy mix and prevent air pollution. In regions with higher level of industrial emissions and air pollution, the initiative to substitute natural gas for coal should be steadily advanced.

References

Ma, B., Cai, H.: How economic globalization affects the happiness of Chinese people: empirical evidence from CGSS 2008. Financ Trade Econ. **7**, 116–127 (2014)

Pan, C.: Equal Opportunities and Social Welfare: Re-investigating of China's Easterlin Paradox. Shanghai People's Publishing House, Shanghai (2019)

Zhu, T.: The past seventy years and prospect of China's energy industry. China Economist **1**, 34–65 (2019)

Chapter 9
Infrastructure and Economic Growth: From the Perspective of New Infrastructure

Zhou was an ancient state, but King Wen adhered to the mandate of Heaven for renovation.
—Book of Songs.

New infrastructure will not only help prevent and control epidemics and stimulate investment and consumption, but also transform the economy. Through econometric analysis by building and calculating a New Infrastructure Development Policy Index (NIDP), this research finds that the development of new infrastructure significantly contributes to regional economic growth and increases TFP. However, in regions where economic development is relative weak, any blind drive to develop new infrastructure may be counterproductive.

9.1 Motivation

9.1.1 Challenges Facing the Chinese Economy

In recent years, profound changes have taken place in China's domestic and the international economic environment. After the global financial crisis in 2008, the world has suffered from a slow economic recovery, rising trade protectionism and unilateralism. In order to boost the domestic economy and create jobs, the United States and other developed countries have implemented policies to bring back manufacturing businesses. In order to maintain its international competitiveness, the UK chose to leave the European Union to reduce burdens on the government. For a while, the idea of "counter-globalization" swept across the world.

Domestically, China has come to a critical period of economic development when the country must simultaneously deal with the slowdown in economic growth, make difficult structural adjustments, and absorb the effects of previous economic stimulus policies, or in other words the Chinese economy has entered a new normal state of development. In the post-crisis era, China's economic growth rate dropped from 9.7% in 2008 to 6. 9% in 2017. Since 2018, trade tension has escalated between the

C. Pan, *Urban Infrastructure and Economic Development in China*, Public Economy and Urban Governance in China, https://doi.org/10.1007/978-981-99-6629-5_9

U.S. and China, which harms China's export and employment and partly accounts for China's economic slowdown. China's economic growth rates in 2018 and 2019 were 6. 7% and 6. 1%, reaching all-time lows since 1991. In this context, transforming economic development and creating new economic drivers are essential to adapt to the new normal conditions and to achieve high-quality development.

In 2020, the unexpected outbreak of COVID-19 disrupted the economic and social development of China. The manufacturing Purchasing Managers' Index (PMI) declined to 35.7 in February 2020; in the first quarter, China's GDP fell by 6.8% year on year, with the output of the primary, secondary, and tertiary sectors falling by 3.2%, 9.6% and 5.2% respectively; and the total profits of industrial enterprises above designated size were 781.45 billion RMB yuan, down 36.7% year on year.[1] Luckily, China handled most difficulties effectively, and industrial production recovered fast.

The worse problem is that the pandemic has swept across the world, most notably Europe and North America. Although governments have taken measures to control the pandemic in their own countries, it is still unclear when it will end. The global economic downturn caused by the pandemic has further dragged down China's economy, and many export-oriented businesses could not resume production as their orders were canceled. In short, China's economy is faced with unprecedented challenges.

9.1.2 Challenges Facing Development of New Infrastructure

Now, a new wave of technological and industrial revolution is surging around the world, which will reshape the global politics and economy. As part of this technological revolution, digital technologies centered around the Internet, such as big data, artificial intelligence, mobile Internet, and cloud computing, have emerged and found their way into the real economy. These nearly invisible forces are demonstrating their enormous power to change the way of production and life and drive economic and social development.

In December 2018, China's Central Economic Working Conference emphasized the need to accelerate 5G commercialization and strengthen the construction of new infrastructure such as artificial intelligence, industrial Internet, and the IoT. The State Council's Report on the Work of the Government in 2019 also emphasized the need to further develop next-generation information infrastructure. In early 2020, facing the COVID-19 outbreak, the central government proposed to "accelerate the construction of new infrastructure projects, such as 5G networks and data centers". On April 17,

[1] GDP for the first quarter of 2020 initial accounting results. http://www.gov.cn/xinwen/202004/18/content_5503803.htm.

2020, CPC General Secretary Xi Jinping chaired a meeting of the Central Political Bureau, emphasizing the need to scale up new infrastructure investment.[2]

In the worst days of the pandemic, new infrastructure did a good job in updating the COVID-19 situation, moderating the mobility of people, and allocating medical resources efficiently. The online work and schooling models, as well as online commerce and government services, played a significant role in resuming social and economic operations. In this way, new infrastructure can help stimulate investment and consumption in the short term, thus accelerating economic recovery. In the long run, integration between new infrastructure and traditional manufacturing can not only improve production efficiency and product quality, but also drive the development of related industries, thus boosting the supply-side structural reform. In short, the development of new infrastructure not only eases burdens on China's economy in the short term, but also helps create a new momentum and facilitate economic transformation in the longer term.

In fact, amid China's economic slowdown and structural transformation, local governments have started to explore the possibilities of new industries based on new infrastructure in order to find and cultivate new paths to grow their economy. This research calculates the frequency of expressions and terms related to "new infrastructure" in each province's annual government work report to build the index NIDP[3] to measure their commitment and efforts to develop new infrastructure. Figure 9.1 illustrates the changes of NIDP in China: from 2008 to 2019, NIDP rose from 42 to 434, with an average annual growth rate of 23.65%, which is much faster than the economic growth rate. That means local governments have been paying closer attention to and investing more heavily in the development of new infrastructure.

9.1.3 Research Questions

Concerning the effects of new infrastructure on economic development, there are several questions: Whether the development of new infrastructure has contributed to regional economic growth? Since improving TFP is the key to realizing economic transformation and endogenous economic growth, how much has the development of new infrastructure raised regional TFP? Does the effect of new infrastructure on economic growth differ between regions at different levels of development? And whether traditional infrastructure can still contribute to regional economic growth and TFP? These are the questions that this research aims to answer.

As said above, this research builds an NIDP index by calculating the frequency of words related to "new infrastructure" in the government work reports of each province over the years, and explores the impact of new infrastructure development

[2] The Standing Committee of the Political Bureau of CPC held a meeting chaired by General Secretary Xi Jinping to consider priorities in strengthening pandemic response and stabilizing economic and social operations. http://www.gov.cn/xinwen/202003/04/content_5486931.htm.

[3] Refer to Sect. 9.3 for the method of constructing NIDP.

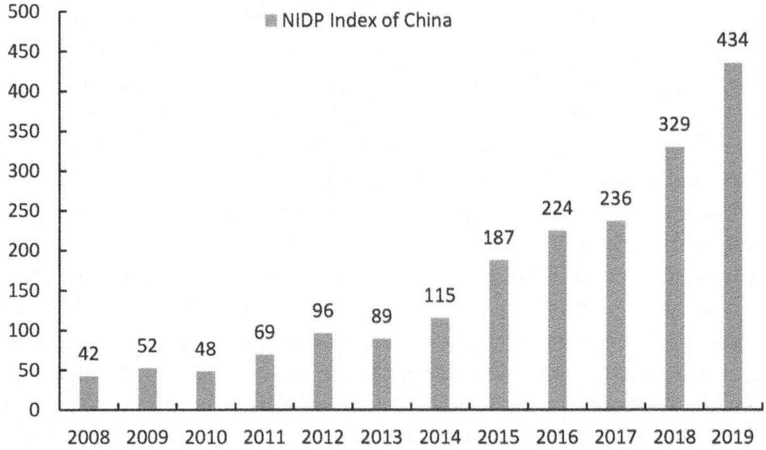

Fig. 9.1 Changes of China's new infrastructure development policy index. *Source* Based on China's provincial annual government work reports

on regional economic growth, especially on regional TFP, by using the panel data of these provinces from 2008 to 2018 and an evidence-based standard economic growth model.

This research has both theoretical and policy implications, giving insights into the endogenous dynamics of China's economic growth, especially the determinants of TFP during the downturn, and contributing to the design and adjustment of new infrastructure-related government policies that aim at creating an endogenous driver for China's high-quality economic development. Besides, this research provides a good reference for empirical studies on economic growth in developing countries.

9.2 Definition of New Infrastructure and Literature Review

9.2.1 Definition of New Infrastructure

New infrastructure is an evolving concept, and there is no clear-cut distinction between the types of new infrastructure and old infrastructure. However, according to the outcome of the Central Economic Work Conference in December 2018, new infrastructure includes four broad categories: 5G, artificial intelligence, industrial Internet, and IoT, while according to the outcome document of a Central Political Bureau meeting in March 2020, new infrastructure involves 5G networks and data centers. Therefore, judging from these authoritative sources, new infrastructure includes five components: artificial intelligence, industrial Internet, IoT, 5G mobile communications network, and data centers, which serves as the definition of new infrastructure in this research.

Some official media have also interpreted the concept of new infrastructure. CCTV says new infrastructure refers to high-tech infrastructure projects in seven areas: 5G access, ultra-high voltage power transmission, intercity high-speed rail and intercity rail transit, electric vehicle charging piles, data centers, artificial intelligence, and industrial Internet.

On April 20, 2020, the National Development and Reform Commission (NDRC) provided the first formal explanation of the term "new infrastructure". New infrastructure has three pillars: the first is information infrastructure which mainly refers to infrastructure projects based on evolving information technologies, e.g., 5G mobile communications, IoT, industrial Internet, satellite Internet; new technology infrastructure projects, e.g., artificial intelligence, cloud computing, and block chain; and computing facilities like data centers and intelligent computing centers; the second is integrated infrastructure which involve the application of Internet, big data, artificial intelligence and other technologies to support the transformation and upgrading of traditional infrastructure, e.g., intelligent transportation and intelligent energy infrastructure; and the third is innovation infrastructure which refers to public infrastructure projects that support scientific research, technology development and product development, e.g., major technology infrastructure, science and education infrastructure, and industrial technology innovation infrastructure.

9.2.2 Economic Attributes of New Infrastructure

From the interpretations and explanations above, new infrastructure has three economic attributes as follows:

First, new infrastructure has the attributes of both private and public goods. As a product, new infrastructure is more private than public, produced and provided by businesses at fair market prices, while traditional infrastructure such as transportation, communication, energy, and water has more public color. Nevertheless, when provided free of charge or at low prices, new infrastructure has the characteristic of public goods.

Secondly, new infrastructure has wide industrial influences and implications. New infrastructure not only involves IT and other high-tech industries, but also many advanced manufacturing and service industries, and covers both upstream and downstream links in their supply chains. In this sense, the development of new infrastructure can help multiple industries, businesses, and operations save costs through the "chain effect", thus boosting the development of entire industrial chains. Therefore, new infrastructure influences and fuels a wide range of industries.

Third, new infrastructure involves high investment risks, so governments must take a cautious attitude towards new infrastructure development. In terms of technology maturity, the core technologies associated with new infrastructure are still in their infancy or childhood, so to speak, so investments in new infrastructure are not only capital-intensive but also risky. When promoting investments in new infrastructure projects, the government should be cautious, respecting market realities and the choice of entrepreneurs, scientists and venture investors, and refrain from making arbitrary or ill-informed decisions.

9.3 Construction of NIDPs

Judging from the above analysis, the government obviously plays a fundamental role in the production and provision of new infrastructure. In fact, since around 2008, Chinese local governments have started to promote and invest in new infrastructure-related industries, and have made substantial progresses. In this sense, government work reports published by each province every year are important sources of information concerning the progress of new infrastructure development in each province. In these reports, governments not only review the regional economic development over the past year, but also announce their development plan, including major initiatives, for the coming year, so these official documents reflect the level of commitment of local governments to new infrastructure development.

To create NIDPs, the first task is to list the terms related to main types of new infrastructure as defined by the central government (see Table 9.1 for the 22 terms). Then, the frequency of these terms in the government work reports of each province in each year is counted and added up to be the NIDP of each province for each year.

Figure 9.2 shows the movement of provincial NIDPs in four major regions of China: Eastern, Northeastern, Central, and Western China. The NIDPs of these four regions are calculated first, and then divided by the number of provinces in each region to obtain the provincial average NIDP. As this figure shows, from 2008 to 2019, the average provincial NIDP rises remarkably in all regions, though the speed varies from region to region (27%, 24%, 23% and 13% in Western, Central, Eastern and Northeastern China respectively). In short, the construction of NIDPs creates

Table 9.1 Terms related to new infrastructure

No.	Terms	No.	Terms
1	5G	12	IoT
2	IT	13	IoT private network
3	Big data	14	New infrastructure
4	Industrial internet	15	Information industry
5	AI	16	Information infrastructure
6	Businesses entering cloud	17	IT
7	Data platform	18	Mobile telecommunication
8	Data center(s)	19	Cloud services
9	Digitization	20	Cloud computing
10	Digital economy	21	Use of cloud services
11	Digital technologies	22	Smart city

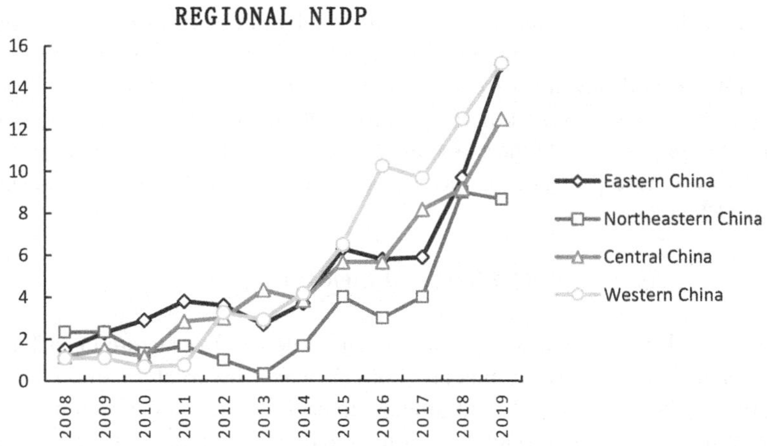

Fig. 9.2 Provincial average NIDPs in four regions of China

an important condition for examining the effects of new infrastructure on economic development.

9.4 Empirical Research Methodology

9.4.1 Theoretical Analysis and Model Setting

Assume that the production function for each of the above-said regions coincides with the Cobb–Douglas production function, and include not only capital and labor as factors of production in the function, but also the regional human capital status which reflects the quality of labor, following the method of Lucas (1988). Then, the production function for each region is:

$$Y_{it} = A_{it} K_{it}^{\alpha} L_{it}^{\beta} E_{it}^{\gamma} \tag{9.1}$$

In which i is the region (province, autonomous region, or municipality directly under the central government); t is the year; and K_{it} is the capital stock; L_{it} is the quantity of labor; E_{it} is the quality of labor or the level of human capital; α, β, and γ are the coefficients of output elasticity; and A_{it} is TFP which stand for factors contributing to economic growth other than the quantity and quality of capital and labor.

Generally speaking, there are two sources of TFP: advances in production technology which creates more output from a given input, and improvements in resource allocation, i.e., channeling scarce resources to places with higher marginal productivity. This study believes that new infrastructure contributes to the increase of TFP.

First, they reduce the marginal cost of production by integrating digital technologies into the production process, thus enabling technological advances to play their role in production. Second, new infrastructure increases the efficiency of resource allocation by reducing the cost of searching and transportation, which allows more resources to be used in production. At the same time, according to the existing literature, traditional infrastructure projects such as roads and energy facilities also contribute to TFP, so TFP is defined as:

$$A_{it} = exp[\theta_1 NIDP_{it} + \theta_2 ln(Rd_{it}) + \rho_i + \sigma_t + u_{it}] \tag{9.2}$$

In which $NIDP_{it}$ measures the development of new infrastructure in each region; $\ln(Rd_{it})$ stands for the development of traditional infrastructure in each region, measured by the logarithm of road mileage in each region; θ_1 is the impact of new infrastructure on economic output; θ_2 is the coefficient of output elasticity of traditional infrastructure; ρ_i and σ_t are fixed effects of province and year; and u_{it} is the error term. After substituting the above TFP definitions into the model and taking the logarithm, the econometric model for this research can be obtained:

$$\begin{aligned} ln(A_{it}) = {} & \alpha ln(K_{it}) + \beta ln(L_{it}) + \gamma ln(E_{it}) + \theta_1 NIDP_{it} + \theta_2 ln(Rd_{it}) \\ & + \rho_i + \sigma_t + u_{it} \end{aligned} \tag{9.3}$$

When other conditions remain unchanged, a one-unit increase in NIDP means a $(100\theta_1)\%$ increase in output and a 1% increase in traditional infrastructure means a $\theta_2\%$ increase in output. Estimates are computed for the above model using the fixed effects of region and year.

9.4.2 *Variable Construction and Data Sources*

(1) Output

Output is the explained variable in this model and is measured as the log of regional GDP deflated by the price index (with 2010 as the base year) of each region.

(2) Factors of production

Capital stock is an important factor of production. Capital stock of each region is measured by the method of Zhang et al. (2004). The dynamic equation for calculating capital stock is:

$$K_{it} = I_{it} + (1 - \delta)K_{it-1} \tag{9.4}$$

In which I_{it} is the investment, and δ is the rate of capital depreciation.

Assume the following: first, total investment in fixed assets (in 100 million RMB yuan) in each region is used to measure investment I_{it}; second, capital stock is derived for the base year of 2000 (K_i) given that the ratio of investment in fixed assets to capital stock is 0.10; and third, the capital depreciation rate δ is 9.6%. Based on these assumptions, the capital stock of each region for the base period is calculated, and then capital stock $K_{it}(t = 2000, \ldots, 2018)$ for each region from 2000 to 2018 is calculated.

Quantity of labor is another major factor of production, and the number of employed people in urban areas (in 10 thousand) is used to measure the quantity of labor L_{it} in each region. Quality of labor, or the level of human capital, is also a factor of production that contributes to regional economic growth. Since the total years of schooling per capita is not available, the number of students enrolled in higher education per 100,000 population is used to measure the quality of labor E_{it} in each region.

(3) TFP

In this model, TFP has two main components: the first is NIDP which is measured as described in Sect. 9.3, and the second is the development of traditional infrastructure which is measured by the logarithm of road mileage. In fact, there are many other factors that make up TFP which are included in the fixed effects of year and province, as well as error terms.

(4) Data sources

Two main sources of data are used for this research: first, the annual government work reports of China's provinces, based on which NIDPs are calculated; and second, China Statistical Yearbooks from which other provincial variables are obtained.

The variables of output, factors of production, and TFP are shown in Table 9.2.

Table 9.2 Basic statistics

Variables	Variable symbols	Observation	Mean	Standard deviation	Minimum	Maximum
Output	*InY*	341	9.4075	1.0073	6.0141	11.2844
Capital stock	*lnK*	341	10.3875	0.9621	7.2803	12.2871
Quantity of labor	*lnL*	341	4.9725	0.9538	2.6872	7.0045
Quality of labor	*lnE*	341	7.7499	0.3283	6.8763	8.8173
Development of traditional infrastructure	*In(Rd)*	341	2.3903	0.8408	0.1398	3.5013
NIDP	*NIDP*	341	4.3607	5.5774	0	49

9.5 Analysis of Estimation Results

9.5.1 *Estimation Results of the Impact of New Infrastructure on Regional Economic Growth*

Table 9.3 shows the estimation results of models with different variable settings. Model (1) is estimated without NIDPs, Model (2) includes NIDP, and Model (3) has the interaction term between NIDPs and the logarithm of GDP per capita to examine the effect of heterogeneity of NIDPs under different levels of economic development. The value of *F* distribution shows that the models are highly significant overall. From the table above, two points are obvious as follows.

First, NIDP is significantly positive, indicating that the development of new infrastructure significantly contributes to regional economic growth. According to the estimation results of Model (2), for every 1 unit increase in the NIDP of a region, the GDP of the same region will increase by 0.3% while all other variables remain unchanged. This effect cannot be ignored. It is worth noting that the above results are obtained on

Table 9.3 Estimation results of the fixed effects of models with NIDPs

	Model (1)	Model (2)	Model (3)
Explained variable	*InY*		
NIDP		0.0030** [0.0009]	– 0.1047** [0.0246]
NIDP × logarithm of GDP per capita			0.0102*** [0.0023]
lnK	0.3131 *** [0.0481]	0.3229** [0.0474]	0.3747 [0.0475]
lnL	0.0076 [0.0183]	0.0068 [0.0180]	– 0.0083 [0.0178]
lnE	0.1037* [0.0567]	0.0367 [0.0595]	0.0729 [0.0583]
ln(Rd)	0.1612* [0.0775]	0.1566* [0.0763]	0.1540* [0.0741]
Dummy variable of province	Yes	Yes	Yes
Dummy variable of year	Yes	Yes	Yes
Observation	341	341	341
InterclassR^2	0.9537	0.9553	0.9581
F distribution	435.5939	420.5579	419.7911
p-value	0.0000	0.0000	0.0000

Notes
1. ***, **, * correspond to 1%, 5%, and 10% respectively
2. Values in [ ] are robust standard errors
3. The estimation results of constant terms are omitted from the table

the condition that the quantity and quality of capital and labor are controlled, so new infrastructure is an important component of TFP. In other words, the development of new infrastructure is a major endogenous driver of economic growth of China.

Second, the coefficient of road mileage is also significantly positive, which means that traditional infrastructure represented by roads is still a strong driver of economic growth, and that roads are also an important component of TFP. According to the estimation results of Model (2), for every 1% increase in road mileage, the regional GDP will increase by 0.1566%.

The estimation results of the coefficients of other control variables are also interesting. First, capital stock is a good factor to explain economic growth. According to the estimation result of Model (2), for every 1% increase in the capital stock, the regional GDP will increase by 0.322 9%, which indicates that the capital stock is a fundamental driver of economic growth. Second, the coefficient of labor quantity is positive but less insignificant in models (1) and (2), suggesting that the expansion of labor force is no longer an important factor in China's economic growth. Last, the coefficient of labor quality, i.e., the human capital level, is only significantly positive in Model (1), but not in models (2) and (3). This may mean the density of university or college students is not a good indicator of the current level of human capital, but reflects the future level of human capital.

Model (3) further examines the heterogeneity of the growth effects of new infrastructure in regions at different levels of economic development. The finding is that the coefficient of the interaction term between NIDP and the logarithm of GDP per capita is significantly positive, while NIDP is significantly negative. This means that in some regions at high levels of economic development, new infrastructure significantly contributes to economic growth, while in some regions at lower levels of economic development, the growth effects of new infrastructure are weak, or the development of new infrastructure even hinders the growth of regional economy. According to the estimation result of Model (3), positive effects of new infrastructure are only possible when the logarithm of the regional GDP per capita (for the base year of 2010) exceeds 10.26.[4] The above results issue the warning that blind promotion of technology-intensive and human resource-intensive new infrastructure-related industries, regardless of the comparative advantages of different regions, may be counterproductive and may generate a negative force that pulls back economic growth.

9.5.2 Accounting of Regional Economic Growth

Table 9.4 breaks down regional economic growth using standard economic growth accounting methods, thereby calculating the relative contribution of each factor of production and each component of TFP to regional economic growth. As the table

[4] The logarithm of GDP per capita in Yunnan Province in 2017 (with 2010 as the base year) is close to 10.26.

Table 9.4 Economic growth accounting

	Contribution level	Contribution rate (%)
Economic growth	0.0968	100
Capital stock	0.0507	52.36
Quantity of labor	0.0007	0.77
Quality of labor	0.0009	0.96
Production factors		54.09
NIDP	0.0034	3.56
Road mileage	0.0044	4.55
Unobservables	0.0366	37.79
TFP		45.91

shows: first, the contributions of factors of production and TFP to regional economic growth are 54.09 and 45.91%; second, the contribution of factors of production is almost exclusively made by capital stock, while the quantity and quality of labor contribute less than 2%; third, among TFP components, NIDP and road mileage contribute 3.56% and 4.55% to regional economic growth, indicating that both new and traditional infrastructures play indispensable role in economic growth; fourth and last, unobservable factors such as the fixed effects of year and region account for the biggest share of TFP, which implies that the components of TFP require much more research.

9.6 Key Findings and Policy Implications

New infrastructure will not only help prevent and control the COVID-19 pandemic, but will also help stimulate investment and consumption, accelerate economic recovery, and drive economic transformation in the medium to long term. This chapter creates an index NIDP by counting the frequency of words related to new infrastructure in the Government Work Reports of each province over the past years, and make estimation by using provincial panel data from 2008 to 2018 and a standard empirical model of economic growth. The study finds that, overall, the development of new infrastructure significantly promotes regional economic growth and increases TFP. However, in regions at low levels of economic development, the blind development of new infrastructure may harm economic growth.

The research in this chapter reveals the endogenous dynamics of China's economic growth and informs policies aiming to generate growth drivers during economic slowdown and adapt to the new normal conditions of economic development. Based on the findings of this research, three policy recommendations can be made as follows.

First, investment in new infrastructure should be increased according to the comparative advantages of different regions. In regions at high levels of economic development, boasting adequate human capital and a concentration of high-tech industries, the government should promote the development of new infrastructure-related industries through tax incentives, better services, and other means. In regions at lower levels of economic development, on the other hand, the government should not blindly promote investments in new infrastructure, but should focus on traditional manufacturing industries to utilize their own advantages, and embrace mature digital technologies such as big data, intelligence, mobile Internet, and cloud computing to improve the efficiency of manufacturing.

Second, following market laws, governments should be cautious about investing in new infrastructure-related industries. While the development of new infrastructure contributes to economic growth, technologies involved in new infrastructure are not mature enough, many of which are still in their infancy and formative stage, so there are investment risks. As governments are not able to identify the prospects of technologies, so the development of new infrastructure and related industries depends heavily on the market, and governments should trust the judgement of entrepreneurs, scientists, and venture capitalists, and cooperate with private investors. In short, governments can play their roles better based on an effective market.

Third, new infrastructure should play a positive part in urban development. In recent years, China's urbanization has accelerated with the population not only moving from rural to urban areas, but also concentrating in first-tier cities and urban complex centering around first-tier cities. The concentration of population often has many negative externalities, such as traffic congestion, environmental pollution, security and safety issues, and other urban ills, which prevent the positive effects of population concentration from coming into play. New infrastructure-related industries should develop and deliver relevant products that meet the needs of urban development, and at the same time improve the efficiency of resource allocation and address negative externalities by harnessing the power of technologies such as big data, cloud computing, and artificial intelligence, thereby enhancing the government's urban governance capacity.

References

Lucas, R.E.: On the mechanics of economic development. J. Monet. Econ. **22**(1), 3–42 (1988)

Zhang, J., Wu, G., Zhang, J.: Interprovincial physical capital stock estimation in China: 1952–2000. Econ. Res. **10**, 35–44 (2004)

Chapter 10
Impacts of Governance on Infrastructure Provision and Institutional Innovations

A good governance system can prevent bad people from doing bad things, while a bad system can prevent good people from doing good things, and may even turn good people into bad people.
—Deng Xiaoping, Reform of the Party and State's Leadership System

10.1 Introduction

This chapter explores governance as a basis for infrastructure provision and aims to offer policy recommendations for promoting innovations in infrastructure provision in China. First, this chapter presents the international experience of how State governance affects infrastructure provision based on literature survey. Second, by analyzing the data of 138 developing countries, this chapter finds that good governance can help promote the private sector's participation in infrastructure development. Third, this chapter interprets China's governance system and its impact on infrastructure provision, especially the impact of decentralization. Finally, this chapter offers policy recommendations on how to promote the development of infrastructure, focusing on the improvement of governance.

10.2 Governance and Corruption in the Infrastructure Sector

10.2.1 Basic Concepts and Significance of Governance

State governance reflects to a large extent a country's institutional capabilities, and the two sides more often than not complement each other. From the perspective of economic development, governance consists of the core components of the

C. Pan, *Urban Infrastructure and Economic Development in China*, Public Economy and Urban Governance in China, https://doi.org/10.1007/978-981-99-6629-5_10

system that prevails in a society, mainly including the political system (collective decision-making process and restraints on politicians and interest groups), government capacity (the government's ability to provide public goods), and regulatory capacity (government's ability to intervene in, encourage, or deter certain economic activities) (Acemoglu et al. 2008).

Francis Fukuyama, a famous political scientist, believes that "State capacity" has three dimensions: governance capacity, government's functional capacity, and legitimacy basis. He argues that effective provision of public goods such as rule of law, order and infrastructure is a major indicator of a country's governance capacity, and the decisive factor in a country's growth is governance capacity rather than the government's functional capacity. He further insists that the weak state capacity of some developing countries might have led to many serious problems, such as terrorism, the spread of AIDS, and poverty (Fukuyama 2007).

According to the Worldwide Governance Indicators (WGI), governance refers to the sum of traditions and institutions by which a state exercises its power, including the process of selecting, supervising, and changing governments, the ability of governments to formulate and implement good policies, and the respect for the institutions that govern socioeconomic interactions between the State and citizens. (Refer to the website of Worldwide Governance Indicators for more details: https://www.unesco.org/en/world-media-trends/worldwide-governance-indicators-wgi.)

WGI measures a country's governance system and capacity in six dimensions: (1) Control of corruption, which measures the abuse of public power by a government to seek private gains, including corrupt behaviors and situations in which the government is "used" by elites and interest groups; (2) Government effectiveness, which measures the quality of government's public service and administration, its independence from political pressure, the quality of policy formulation and implementation, and the credibility of government commitments; (3) Political stability and absence of violence, which measures the likelihood of a government being destabilized or subverted through unconstitutional or violent means, including politically motivated violence and terrorism; (4) Regulatory quality, which measures the ability of a government to formulate and implement good regulatory rules to promote the development of the private sector; (5) Rule of law, which measures the extent to which people believe in and obey public rules, including rules governing contract enforcement, protection of property rights, security, and justice; and (6) Voice and Accountability, which measures the degree to which a country's citizens participate in selecting their own government, as well as the degree to which freedom of speech, association, and ownership of free media are exercised.

Numerous empirical studies have consistently shown that strong governance can promote investment, innovation, and human capital accumulation, thereby promoting economic growth, while weak governance may lead to abuse of public power, corruption, and economic stagnation.

In a modern society, the development of infrastructure projects such as transportation, communication, energy, and water conservancy depends on public funding, and the process of bidding, procurement and project management will involve the use of public power, so in countries or regions where governance capacity is relatively weak, corruption occurs easily in the infrastructure sector, which not only reduces the efficiency of public investment, but also threatens the final quality of infrastructure. In other words, effective provision of infrastructure, as a public good, is a major indicator of a country's governance capacity.

10.2.2 Historical Lessons: Corruption in the US Infrastructure Sector

Stanley Engerman and Kenneth L. Sokoloff reviewed the history of American infrastructure projects such as the Erie Canal in New York State in the nineteenth century. They used the ratio of actual cost of public works to the original budget ("cost overrun") to measure the extent of corruption and the quality of public governance in building public works. They found that the planning and implementation of the Erie Canal project were appropriate, the project brought huge welfare improvements to New Yorkers, and its actual cost was close to the budget, with the cost overrun standing at a satisfactory ratio of 1.46. The successful implementation of the Erie Canal project encouraged other parts of the United States to invest public funds in building transportation infrastructure. Unfortunately, due to the weakening of cost control and regulation, the final cost of many projects far exceeded their initial budget. In terms of cost overrun, the Mississippi River flood control project (1883–1926) exceeded 20, and the Interstate Highway project (1952–1953) was as high as 19.1, Boston Central Artery/Tunnel Project (1991–2004) came to 5.12. It can be seen how corrupt infrastructure projects can be (Engerman and Sokoloff 2012).

David Cutler and Grant Miller examined the development of municipal finance and water systems in the United States from the early 19th to the early 20th centuries (Cutler and Miller 2012). By analyzing historical data, they found that public ownership of water systems rises rapidly during this period, while the size of waterworks continued to expand. After studying the cases of Boston and New York, they believed that it was because of the development and innovation of local public finance, especially the use of municipal bonds, that municipal governments had financial resources needed to build public waterworks to replace those run by private companies, which ultimately advanced the public interest. In the meantime, government involvement would lead to an increase in corruption, but they argued that corruption in fact went hand in hand with policies that improve public welfare if corrupt politicians seek both political support and a robust economy.

Werner Troesken examined the regulatory history of water, electricity, gas and other municipal utilities in the United States from the 19th century to the mid-to-late twentieth century (Troesken 2012). He found that the development of US municipal utilities shows a cycle going from private supply to public supply and then back to privatization again. He believed that technology and ideology could not account for the above changes, and the transition in regulatory regimes is the fundamental reason for the growth and transformation of public utilities. Based on Mancur Lloyd Olson's theory of institutional ossification, he argued that changes in regulatory regimes could break the original pattern of interests, thereby improving the efficiency of resource allocation. At the same time, he emphasized that corruption is endemic to public utility industries, and regime changes only changed the type of corruption, but did not eliminate corruption.

10.2.3 Corrupted Infrastructure Sector in Developing Countries

Corruption abounds in infrastructure projects in developing countries. For example, in the early 2000s, Biblioteca Vasconcelos of Mexico, a library much hyped once, was forced to close within less than a year after its completion due to structural defects. Many violations were revealed, and the remedy cost the government heavily (Roland 2016). It is precisely due to the lack of governance capacity in some developing countries, especially their weakness in the face of corruption, that private companies chose to pay bribes to government officials in order to win contracts or avoid government regulation. At the same time, under weak governance, the theft of infrastructure building materials, as well as electricity and tap water, is very serious (Olken 2004). All in all, all this would dramatically increase the cost of infrastructure provision and reduce the quality of services.

Charles Kenny, an American economist, studied corruption in the infrastructure sector in developing countries. Kenny (2006) found through surveys and calculations that the cost of corruption in infrastructure investment and maintenance alone in developing countries might equal 18 billion US dollars per year. In India, about 25% of electricity production was lost to illegal connections. In Indonesia, about 24% of funds to be used for road construction "went missing". Surveys of countries in Eastern Europe and Central Asia also showed that bribes paid to government officials amount to about 7% of government contract values. These levels of corruption measured by physical and financial audit, however, were far smaller than perceptions.

Kenny (2007) further examined corruption in the construction sector in developing countries. He pointed out that the construction sector accounted for about one-third of gross capital formation, and in many cases, governments played major roles as clients, regulators, and owners of construction companies at the same time, so this sector was consistently considered as one of the most corrupt. Large payments to gain or alter contracts and circumvent regulations were common. In developing countries such as India, Cameroon, Guatemala, and Lebanon companies needed to pay bribes to government officials to obtain business licenses, building permits and pass inspections for compliance with labor standards. He further noted that in countries with high levels of corruption as measured by Transparency International's Corruption Perceptions Index (CPI), such as Albania, Uganda, and Russia, the cost of road repairs was higher. Corruption not only led to bribery, but also poor-quality construction of infrastructure with low economic returns.

Kenny (2007) pointed out that governance played a central role in attempts to reduce corruption and increase the returns to infrastructure investment, and then proposed a pragmatic reform plan. He insisted that stronger governance capacity can not only encourage private sector investment in projects with longer payback periods, but also help governments improve the management of infrastructure stock. In short, whether infrastructure is in private or public hands, improved governance is necessary.

10.3 Governance and Private Participation in Infrastructure Provision

The theoretical analysis and empirical evidence provided in Sect. 10.1 have shown that weak governance is an ultimate cause of corruption and inadequate infrastructure provision. Therefore, improving governance is a necessary step to improve infrastructure provision. This section further emphasizes that improved governance can also encourage private participation in infrastructure provision, thereby easing the pressure on public finance in developing countries and securing lasting economic development.

10.3.1 Hypotheses

Corruption means the use of public power to seek private gains, especially by government officials. On the surface, both corruption and taxation reduce the yields of economic activities and investments, and thus hinder economic growth. Unlike taxation, corruption is unpredictable, threatens to reduce the quality of public goods and services, and encourages government officials to intervene in the market. Therefore, corruption has a worse impact on resource allocation than taxation (Shleifer and Vishny 1993).

Corruption is the major cost and a common manifestation of poor governance, and the improvement of governance can effectively curb corruption. In infrastructure, improving governance and curbing corruption can not only reduce bribes private firms would have to pay to secure contracts, but also help reduce theft of infrastructure materials and products, thereby increasing the yields of private investments in infrastructure. Meanwhile, effective control of corruption can reduce the chance of governments' default on contracts, thereby improving the attitude of private companies towards signing long-term infrastructure contracts with the government. So, Hypothesis 1 is: Improving governance and controlling corruption can encourage private participation in infrastructure provision.

In what follows, data of 138 developing countries from 1996 to 2014 and econometric models will be used to test Hypothesis 1.

10.3.2 Empirical Research Methodology

(1) Econometric model

The following econometric model is proposed to test Hypothesis 1:

$$ln\ APPI_{ist} = \beta_0 + \beta_1 Gov_{ist} + \beta_2 M_{ist} + \lambda_s + \eta_t + u_{ist} \tag{10.1}$$

In which i is a developing country; s is the continent or region where the country is located; t is the year; $ln\ APPI$ is the level of private participation in infrastructure; Gov is the governance capacity of the country; M_{ist} is a series of country-level control variables; λ_s and η_t are dummy variables of region and period; u_{ist} is the error term; β_0, β_1 and β_2 are constants, in which β_1 measures the impact of governance on private participation in infrastructure provision and thus the focus of this research. In Hypothesis 1, β_1 is bigger than 0. OLS is used to make estimations for the above model.

(2) Explained variable: Private participation in infrastructure (PPI)

Private participation in infrastructure ($ln\ APPI$) is the explained variable of this research. The calculation is as follows: First, based on World Development Indicators' data of investments involving the private sector or private participation in infrastructure (PPI) in five sectors of infrastructure: energy, communication, transportation, water supply and sanitation in developing countries, investments in four sectors are chosen and added up, and then the total investment is deflated using the American GDP deflator for the base period of 2010 and divided by the national population. On this basis, logarithm is taken of per capita investment with private participation in infrastructure projects over the years, namely $lnAPPI$ (in thousand US dollars per person[1]), and this variable is used to measure the level of private participation in infrastructure in a country. Three points must be explained:

First, about the term PPI. According to WDI, the term "private" in "private participation in infrastructure" refers to private companies and foreign-funded companies that participate in infrastructure provision, so it should be understood as the "private sector" instead of "individual persons".

Second, about PPI as a variable. This variable in the WDI database refers to the amount of investment in infrastructure projects with PPI. WDI explains that this "investment" includes the sum of public and private investments, in which the private sector assumes a certain level of risks during the contract period for the building and operation of infrastructure. According to the explanation above, "investment" is not entirely the contribution of the private sector, and PPI does not necessarily mean direct capital expenditures on or partial ownership of infrastructure. For example, under an operation and management contract, the private sector may be involved in infrastructure provision, but does not make any direct investment.

[1] "Thousand dollars per person" is used as the unit here to make the data in Table 10.1 more understandable and make the analysis easier.

Therefore, "private participation in infrastructure provision" is more appropriate than "private participation in infrastructure investment" to describe the role of the private sector in infrastructure. At the same time, this research uses per capita investment with private sector participation (logarithm) to measure the level of private participation in infrastructure provision: the more investment is made in infrastructure with private participation, the more the private sector is involved, or the higher the PPI level is.

Third, cases of zero PPI. In the countries covered in this research, the vast majority (135/138) open their infrastructure sector to private investors, so their PPI is usually positive. However, there are cases where PPI is 0 in some years, and there are a handful of countries whose PPI is 0 in all years, including the Federated States of Micronesia, Solomon Islands, and East Timor. In order to include these cases into the econometric model, $ln\ APPI$ is revised and becomes $ln(APPI + 1)$, so that the logarithm of the cases with zero PPI will remain zero without having to change the monotonicity of PPI.

(3) Core explanatory variable: Governance

Governance (*Gov*) is a core explanatory variable of this research. Corruption control is a key aspect of a country's governance. Therefore, corruption control is used as a variable to evaluate a country's governance based on the WGI database. In this econometric model, for every 1 unit of improvement in corruption control, $ln\ APPI$ will rise by $(100 \cdot \beta_1)\%$.

(4) Control variables

In order to minimize the estimation bias caused by any potential variable omission, the following control variables are also used. First, the level of openness to investment. The ratio of net FDI inflows to GDP is used to measure the level of investment openness in a country. A higher level of investment openness will bring more capital to the country to increase investment in infrastructure, and the entry of multinational companies will also impact the country's governance. Therefore this variable is included in this model. At the same time, the level of trade openness, or the proportion of total import and export to GDP, is also used as a surrogate variable to test the robustness of this model.

Second, Internet penetration. As a modern communication infrastructure, the Internet can affect the dissemination of information in a country and thus affect its governance, while Internet penetration is closely related to infrastructure development, so it is included in this model. In this case, mobile phone penetration is used as a surrogate variable.

Third, contribution of natural resources. Contribution of natural resources refers to the difference between the market price of natural resources (oil, natural gas, coal, minerals, and forests, etc.) and their production cost as a percentage of GDP, which measures the contribution of natural resources to economic growth. Rich natural resources can bring high capital inflows to a country, thereby promoting infrastructure development, but the country may fall into the "resource curse". For this purpose, the contribution of oil is used as a surrogate variable.

Fourth, income group is used as a dummy variable, with countries classified into four income groups: high, upper-middle, lower-middle, and low-income countries. This dummy variable reflects the overall development level of a country.

Fifth, region is also used as a dummy variable. The world is divided into East Asia and the Pacific, South Asia, Europe, and Central Asia, Latin America and the Caribbean, Middle East and North Africa, and Sub-Saharan Africa. By including "region" as a dummy variable, heterogeneity factors such as national geography, climate, and culture can be controlled to a certain extent.

Sixth, period is another dummy variable. This study covers four periods: 1996–2000, 2001–2005, 2006–2010, and 2011–2014. This dummy variable is used to control the time movement of related variables.

(5) Data sources

The data used in this research mainly come from two sources: first, the WGI database, which provides relevant information on corruption control in countries; second, the WDI database, which contains the data of private participation in infrastructure in countries, including amount of investment, level of openness, infrastructure development, and contribution of natural resources.

It should be noted that the 138 developing countries covered in this research are selected based on the World Bank's "Private Participation in Infrastructure" research project, considering the target country's national income per capita and level of infrastructure development. Judging by the World Bank standard (2015 national income per capita), among these countries, except for Chile, Uruguay, Lithuania, Seychelles, Antigua and Barbuda, and The Federation of Saint Kitts and Nevis which are upper-middle-income countries (annual income per capita coming to 12,475 US dollars or more), others are lower-middle-income countries (annual income per capita ranging from 1026 to 12,475 US dollars) and low-income countries (annual income per capita below 1026 US dollars), so the 138 countries can represent "developing countries" as a group.

10.3.3 Analysis of Estimation Results

Table 10.1 shows the results of full-sample OLS estimation of the impact of governance on promoting private participation in infrastructure provision. In this table, Model 1 only uses corruption-controlled univariate to perform regression, Model 2 adopts three dummy variables: income group, region and period, and Model 3 introduces other control variables. According to the F distribution, each model is highly significant. It can be seen from the table that the coefficient of corruption control is significantly positive. The above correlation can be interpreted as a causal effect, indicating that corruption control significantly promotes private participation in infrastructure, which supports Hypothesis 1.

Estimates of coefficients of the control variables are enlightening. First, the coefficient of investment openness is significantly positive. This may be because some

Table 10.1 Results of full-sample OLS estimation of the effect of governance on promoting private participation in infrastructure provision

	Model 1	Model 2	Model 3
Explained variable	ln*APPI*		
Corruption control	0.0180*** [0.0020]	0.0090*** [0.0019]	0.0079*** [0.0024]
Investment openness			0.0722*** [0.0234]
Internet penetration			0.0306** [0.0124]
Contribution of natural resources			– 0.0107*** [0.0037]
Low-income country		– 0.0295*** [0.0092]	– 0.0506*** [0.0124]
Lower-middle-income country		– 0.0235*** [0.0089]	– 0.0455*** [0.0121]
Upper-middle-income countries		– 0.0072 [0.0089]	– 0.0314*** [0.0120]
Region as a dummy variable	No	Yes	Yes
Period as a dummy variable	No	Yes	Yes
Observation	2706	2706	2338
Adjusted R^2	0.0420	0.113 8	0.1499
F distribution	81.5711	39.4492	30.3412
p-value	0.0000	0.0000	0.0000

Notes
1. ***, **, * indicate the significance levels of 1%, 5%, and 10% respectively
2. Values in [ ] are robust standard errors
3. Estimation results of dummy variables and constant terms for "region" and "period" are omitted from the table

foreign-funded companies have also participated in infrastructure, driven by the inflow of FDI. Second, the coefficient of Internet penetration is also significantly positive. This suggests that improvements in communications infrastructure have in turn helped the private sector to participate in infrastructure provision. Third, the coefficient of natural resource contribution is significantly negative. This means that, in a country endowed with abundant natural resources, the private sector would be more eager for opportunities in resource-based industries while ignoring infrastructure, which may explain why some resource-based countries have been caught by the "resource curse". Fourth, the estimation results of the dummy variable of "income group" indicate that, while other variables are constant, the level of private participation in infrastructure continues to decline as the country's income level rises. In Model 3, lnAPPI is about 5% lower in low-income countries than high-income countries (the base group).

Table 10.2 shows the OLS estimation results after substituting control variables and deleting samples with zero PPI. Among them, "investment openness", "Internet penetration" and "contribution of natural resources" are replaced with "trade openness", "mobile phone penetration" and "contribution of oil" respectively. The estimation results of Model 4 show that corruption control significantly promotes private participation in infrastructure. Compared with the estimates of Model 3, the estimated coefficient of corruption control is significantly magnified. For every 0.1 unit of improvement in corruption control, the logarithm of per capita private investment in infrastructure will rise by 7.323%. This result again validates Hypothesis 1, and shows that including a zero-PPI sample in the model may significantly underestimate the positive effect of corruption control.

In conclusion, Hypothesis 1 is tested and confirmed by the above transnational empirical research: the improvement of a country's governance, or its corruption control, can promote the participation of the private sector in infrastructure provision.

Table 10.2 Robustness of governance in promoting private participation in infrastructure

	Model 4
Explained variable	ln*APPI*
Corruption control	0.7323*** [0.0863]
Trade openness	0.012 [0.1243]
Mobile phone penetration	0.9440*** [0.1367]
Contribution of oil	0.4532 [0.4160]
Low-income country	− 0.0297 [0.2736]
Lower-middle-income country	0.2183 [0.2288]
Upper-middle-income countries	0.6340*** [0.1992]
Region as a dummy variable	No
Period as a dummy variable	No
Observation	1402
Adjusted R^2	0.349
F distribution	54.8177
P-value	0.0000

Notes

1. ***, **, * indicate the significance levels of 1%, 5%, and 10% respectively.
2. Values in [ ] are robust standard errors.
3. Estimation results of dummy variables and constant terms for "region" and "period" are omitted from the table.

This conclusion supports the relationship between a country's governance capacity and infrastructure provision, and offers a clue for alleviating the funding shortage for infrastructure development in developing countries. However, this research does not intend to limit governance to corruption control only. Indeed, it is also necessary to examine the impacts of other dimensions of governance on private participation in infrastructure provision, which is one of the key tasks of future research.

10.4 State Governance, Decentralization, and Infrastructure Provision

10.4.1 State Governance and the Two "Centenary Goals"

As Chinese President Xi Jinping once said: "State governance capacity reflects to a large extent a country's institutional capacity. China's national governance system is an institutional system that governs the development of the country under the leadership of the Party, encompassing mechanisms, administrative, legal, and regulatory arrangements for economic, political, cultural, social, environmental development and Party building. It is, in other words, a system of closely linked and coordinated rules. State governance capacity is the ability to use this system to manage all aspects of social affairs, including reform, development and stability, internal affairs, foreign affairs and national defense, and governance of the Party, the country, and the military." (The Publicity Department of the Central Committee of the CPC 2019) This important remark contains a very good definition of State governance.

No doubt, governance is a core part of a country's institutional system. Institutional advantage is the defining advantage of a country, and institutional competition is the key area of competition among countries. If its institutional system is stable, the country would be stable. Social harmony and long-term stability of China depend on our institutional system, our governance capacity, and the competence of government officials. To capture the institutional advantage of socialism with Chinese characteristics, China must modernize its governance system in all aspects (The Publicity Department of the Central Committee of the CPC 2019). The Decision on Major Issues Concerning Comprehensively Deepening Reform adopted by the Third Plenary Session of the 18th CPC Central Committee of the CPC clearly stated that the goal of deepening the reform is to further develop socialism with Chinese characteristics, and to promote the modernization of China's governance system and capacity.

According to the Decision of the CPC Central Committee on Major Issues Concerning Upholding and Improving the System of Socialism with Chinese Characteristics and Advancing the Modernization of China's System and Capacity for Governance, which was adopted by the 4th Plenary Session of the 19th Central Committee of the CPC: "The goal of upholding and improving the system of socialism with Chinese characteristics and advancing the modernization of China's system and capacity for governance is that: by the centenary of our Party, the system will be more mature and institutionalized in all aspects; by 2035, the system will be more perfect in all aspects, and the modernization of China's system and capacity for governance will be basically realized; by the centenary of the People's Republic of China, the modernization of China's system and capacity for governance will be fully realized, so the system of socialism with Chinese characteristics will be more solid and its superiority will be fully shown."

10.4.2 Chinese Decentralization as a Form of State Governance

The division of power between China's central and local governments is a key feature of China's governance system. Judging from the existing literature, scholars generally agree that the Chinese style of decentralization is defined by the seamless combination of economic decentralization and political centralization, which is a key institutional arrangement and a key driver of China's rapid economic growth.

Qian and Weingast (1997), using the "new firm theory" in their study of public economics, proposed the second-generation theory of fiscal federalism, and answered why local government officials were motivated to provide public goods and maintain the market order in the course of China's reform and opening up, while they are free from massive corruption and bribery. They believe that China's decentralization has produced two "incentives".

The first incentive derives from information and power delegation. On one hand, the central government has authorized local governments to develop and implement their own fiscal and financial policies, thereby enhancing their readiness to develop local economy, which in turn limits the central government's control over local governments. On the other hand, the central government is no longer able to rescue all failing business enterprises, which makes it necessary to mobilize local governments to take care of SOEs and township or village enterprises, while limiting the control of local government over enterprises, because local governments depend on taxes paid by companies to fulfill their obligation to provide public goods and services.

The other incentive comes from regional competition. Under the institutional arrangement of economic decentralization, local governments have worked aggressively to attract factors of production (to form the tax base). As the movable tax base tends to leave any "bad government" and flow into a region with a "good government", the local government's control is effectively limited. At the same time, regional competition increases the opportunity cost of saving failing enterprises, because it is less efficient or effective to use financial resources to save enterprises than to use them to provide public goods to attract foreign investment. This competition endogenously hardens the budget constraints on local government.

Qian and Roland (1998) established a game model and argued that under the framework of decentralization, China's central government not only cares about the political performance of local governments, but also pays close attention to their economic performance, so local governments are less motivated to bail out state-owned enterprises facing bankruptcy or struggling to with their poor performance than to attract the inflow of factors by improving infrastructure.

Blanchard and Shleifer (2001) believed that while China's central government gave local governments more and more financial autonomy, they kept effective political control over local governments. That means China administers a combination of economic decentralization and political centralization. On the other hand, Russia's central government has weak control over local governments, so local governments have no incentive to promote local economic development.

Zhou (2007) described China's decentralization as a "promotion tournament" for local officials. He believed that this institutional arrangement of China combining fiscal decentralization and vertical political control, especially the method of official performance evaluation based on local economic growth, will directly cause local officials to unilaterally pursuing local economic development in order to get promoted, or increase their chance of getting promoted. While this institutional arrangement plays a part in driving local economic growth, it also encourages local governments to ignore individual people's well-being and environmental well-being, and take non-cooperative gaming actions such as implementing local protection and erecting market barriers.

Xu (2011) labeled China's decentralization as a case of Regionally Decentralized Authoritarianism (RDA). He believed that in China's RDA regime, there is political centralization on one hand, where the central government appoints officials from the top down and rotates officials, while there is also economic decentralization on the other, where local governments control land use rights, enterprises, financial revenues, and energy and other factors of production. The RDA regime encourages local governments to carry out economic experiments, such as the household contract responsibility system, township and village enterprises, special economic zones, and the ownership restructuring of state-owned enterprises, all of which are reforms realized from the bottom up. At the same time, the RDA regime also encourages local and regional competition. Local governments work hard to attract investment and promote economic growth through land use right transfer, tax relief, infrastructure investment, and administrative system reform, while the central government evaluates the performance of local government officials based on GDP growth and FDI inflows. He argued that China's RDA regime has a positive effect in promoting economic growth, but this regime is not effective when the government is obliged to fulfill multiple goals, such as achieving economic growth and environmental protection at the same time.

10.4.3 *Impact of Chinese-Style Decentralization on Infrastructure Provision*

Some scholars have explored the impact of decentralization on infrastructure provision in China. Zhang et al (2007) found that, when evaluating a country's institutional arrangements, the academia tends to emphasize the "soft" side such as the political system. Thus, they would praise India, which has inadequate infrastructure but implements democratic elections, ignoring whether the government is effective on the "hard" side, such as infrastructure development and provision. They hold that the performance of local governments in providing infrastructure depends on its political system. In China, the central government conducts top-down political management and evaluates the performance of local government officials based on economic growth, while local governments have the motivation to improve infrastructure provision to attract investment in order to win the "competition".

Fu and Zhang (2007) believed that China's fiscal decentralization and competition between governments driven by performance evaluation have distorted the public spending's of local governments, who focus too much on infrastructure building but neglect investment in human capital or public services, while inter-government competition exacerbates the distorting effect of fiscal decentralization on government expenditure. Similarly, Sun and Pan (2009) found that China's fiscal decentralization significantly expanded the expenditures of local governments on infrastructure, science, education, culture, and public health, as well as administrative expenses, in which the impact on infrastructure spending is the biggest. In a word, Chinese-style decentralization has motivated local governments to invest more actively in infrastructure provision.

10.5 Impact of Improved Governance on Infrastructure Provision

Based on international experience, transnational empirical and theoretical analysis, this chapter explores the impact of State governance on infrastructure provision. The research has produced three conclusions: first, in a given country, weakness of governance underlies corruption and inefficient use of public funds in the infrastructure sector; second, improved governance in developing countries can help attract private capital to the infrastructure sector, thereby promoting economic development; third, China's institutional system characterized by the combination of political centralization and economic decentralization, which is the core of China's governance institution, would strongly motivate local governments to provide infrastructure, and create the institutional basis for China to realize rapid economic growth.

In a word, enhancing its governance and improving the decentralization arrangement are essential for effective infrastructure provision in China. The following policy recommendations are based on these conclusions.

First, the unified leadership of the central government must be maintained and the administration of government officials must improve. The reform of government official evaluation should be advanced. While they select and appoint officials with both political integrity and competence, under the principle of using the best people from all over the world, governments should include effective provision of public goods such as infrastructure as a key dimension in official performance evaluation. GDP growth must not remain the only criterion, but more attention should be paid to how local government officials promote economic transformation and whether they can create a new economic momentum. This would encourage local government officials to provide infrastructure, bring innovations to infrastructure provision, and accelerate infrastructure development.

Second, the power and duty division between central and local governments must be more clearly defined to motivate local governments. The central government should strengthen its role in macro control, maintain the integrity of the national legal system, the government, and the market, and ensure cross-regional infrastructure provision. At the same time, it is necessary to give local governments more autonomy in the development of traditional and new infrastructure, support local governments to work creatively according to local actual conditions and comparative strengths, in order to improve the efficiency of resource allocation. On this basis, a proper fiscal relationship should be built between the central government and local governments with a clear power and responsibility division to guarantee appropriate allocation of financial resources and regional balance, so that the expenditure responsibility of governments at all levels can be well supported by their financial resources.

Third, proper corruption prevention mechanisms should be built to safeguard innovations in infrastructure provision. This chapter finds that enhancing corruption control in a country can help attract the private sector to participate in infrastructure provision, thereby reducing the financial pressure on the government and promoting innovations in infrastructure provision. The Report to the 19th National Congress of the CPC pointed out that since the 18th National Congress of the CPC, China has created and maintained a strong momentum of anti-corruption drive. Now, it is still necessary to further advance the fight against corruption, build an integrated system to ensure that officials dare not, cannot, and do not want to be corrupt, and develop a system of regulatory rules governing the sector of public works including infrastructure.

References

Acemoglu, D., Rodrik, D., North, D., Fukuyama, F.: Governance, growth, and development decision-making. Comparative Studies. CITIC Press Group, Beijing (2008)

Blanchard, O., Shleifer, A.: Federalism with and without political centralization: China versus Russia. IMF Staff Papers, **48**, 171–179 (2001)

Cutler, D., Miller, G.: Water, water everywhere: municipal finance and water supply in American cities. In: Glaeser, E.L., Goldin, C. (eds.) Corruption and Reform: Lessons from America's

Economic History. Translated by Hu Jiayong and Wang Zhaobin. Commercial Press, Beijing (2012)

Engerman, S., Sokoloff, K.L.: Digging the dirt at public expense: governance in the building of the Erie Canal and other public works. In: Glaeser, E.L., Goldin, C. (eds.) Corruption and Reform: Lessons from America's Economic History. Translated by Hu Jiayong and Wang Zhaobin. Commercial Press, Beijing (2012)

Fu, Y., Zhang, Y.: Chinese decentralization and fiscal expenditure bias: the costs of competing for growth. Management World **3**, 4–12, 22 (2007)

Fukuyama, F.: State-building: Governance and World Order in the 21st Century (trans: by Huang Shengqiang, Xu Mingyuan). China Social Sciences Press, Beijing (2007)

Kenny, C.: Measuring and reducing the impact of corruption in infrastructure. World Bank Working Paper, No. 4099 (2006)

Kenny, C.: Construction, corruption, and developing countries. World Bank Working Paper, No. 4271 (2007)

Olken, B.: Monitoring corruption: evidence from a field experiment in Indonesia. NBER Working Paper, No. 11753 (2004)

Qian, Y., Weingast, B.R.: Federalism as a commitment to preserving market incentives. J. Econ. Perspect. **11**(4), 83–92 (1997)

Qian, Y., Roland, G.: Federalism and the soft budget constraint. Am. Econ. Rev. **88**(5), 1143–1162 (1998)

Roland, G.: Development Economics (trans: Jin Zhinong). Renmin University of China Press, Beijing (2016)

Shleifer, A., Vishny, R.W.: Corruption. Q. J. Econ. **108**(3), 599–617 (1993)

Sun, L., Pan, C.: The Leviathan hypothesis: fiscal sharing and the expansion of local governments – based on provincial evidence from 1998 to 2006. Collected Essays on Finance and Economics **2** (2009)

The Publicity Department of the Central Committee of the Communist Party of China. An Outline for Studying Xi Jinping Thought on Socialism with Chinese Characteristics for a New Era. Learning Press Limited, Beijing (2019)

Troesken, W.: Regime change and corruption: a history of public utility regulation. In: Glaeser, E.L., Goldin, C. (eds.) Corruption and Reform: Lessons from America's Economic History. Translated by Hu Jiayong and Wang Zhaobin. Commercial Press, Beijing (2012)

Xu, C.: The fundamental institutions of China's reforms and development. J. Econ. Lit. **49**(4), 1076–1151 (2011)

Zhang, J., Gao, Y., Fu, Y.: Why Does China have good infrastructure? Econ. Res. J. **3**, 4–19 (2007)

Zhou, L.: A study on the promotion competition of local Chinese government officials. J. Econ. Res. **7** (2007)

The manufacturer's authorised representative in the EU is Springer Nature Customer Service Centre GmbH, Europaplatz 3, 69115 Heidelberg, Germany. If you have any concerns regarding our products, please contact ProductSafety@springernature.com

Printed and bound by CPI Group (UK) Ltd, Croydon, CR0 4YY
30/09/2026
02225264-0018